Aaron Warford

How to dress: For ladies and gentlemen

The art of selecting and arranging colors to suit any complexion and figure

fully explained

Aaron Warford

How to dress: For ladies and gentlemen
The art of selecting and arranging colors to suit any complexion and figure fully explained

ISBN/EAN: 9783337223809

Hergestellt in Europa, USA, Kanada, Australien, Japan

Cover: Foto ©Lupo / pixelio.de

Weitere Bücher finden Sie auf **www.hansebooks.com**

HOW TO DRESS.

FOR LADIES AND GENTLEMEN.

The art of selecting and arranging colors to
suit any complexion and figure
fully explained.

ALSO,

EFUL INSTRUCTION

TING MATERIAL FOR DRESSES, HOW TO MAKE THEM.
AND WHAT TO WEAR WHILE TRAVELING
AND AT HOME.

NEW YORK:
NK TOUSEY, Publisher,
34 AND 36 NORTH MOORE STREET.

HOW TO DRESS.

MATERIALS OF DRESS.

IT must not be supposed from the heading of this chapter that we are going to inflict upon the reader a long account of silks, satins, velvets, and the thousand and one materials which have been invented to furnish the infinite variety in ladies' dresses. We refer to the subject chiefly to indicate the necessity that exists, in applying the laws of color, for considering the substance, surface, and texture of which the dress is composed.

Materials which are rough in surface, or absorbent in texture, are very differently affected by the rays of light from those which are smooth and lustrous, and the colors they exhibit are different in themselves, and produce a different effect upon the eye. A piece, of crimson satin, for example, would differ in color and in effect from a piece of crimson silk, although of like intensity. of tone, and, in fact, dyed with it in the same vat; each, again, would differ still more from a piece of velvet, merino, or tarletan, although all were as similar as the art of the dyer could make them.

In some colors the difference of value according to the material would be very marked and decisive. . A yellow satin might be superb, where the same yellow in cloth would be simply detestable. And not only does the character of the color depend on the absorbent or reflective condition of the surface, but also very much of the accidental effects produced by play of light and shade, contact with other colors, and the like.

Thus, in a strong light, while the parts of a rich satin dress, which catch the brightest light, are glittering and almost colorless, the folds exhibit almost every possible difference of tone, from the shadows being broken by the reciprocal reflections of the opposite parts. The same thing will be noticed in a less degree with silks; differently with velvets, yet producing the most beautiful effects, as any one may see who will condescend to study such details. In merino or cashmere the effect is very different again, the broken lights and reflections being almost lost in the absorbent character of the material.

Further, texture may be considered with reference to contrast as well as to color. Thus, almost intuitively, the milliner and dressmaker prefer to trim the glossy satins and silks with an absorbent velvet; the dull merino or cashmere with the richer velvet, or glossy silk or satin.

Again, the rough crapes and laces are placed in contact with the skin, and never with so much advantage as when the skin is smooth, polished, and pearly; never with so little as when the pearliness is produced by powder.

The effect of the material, in respect to color, is further modified by the circumstance of its having a plain or a figured surface. If the pattern be merely raised, it chiefly affects the quality of the texture, its smoothness, or otherwise. If it be a colored design, it necessarily influences the general harmony, and must be taken into account in considering the trimmings, and other details of the dress. Patterns, if well designed, may add greatly to the richness and elegance of the dress, but, unfortunately, they are not often well designed, and much as the superiority of the French designer is vaunted, and in some matters very justly, it is undeniable that many of the most outrageous patterns are of French designing. The reader may remember the rapture with which Ruskin, in his "Stones of Venice," speaks of the patterns on the dresses introduced in Venetian pictures, and particularly in those by Tintoretto. There can be little doubt that they were copies from actual silks worn by Venetian ladies, but they must have been designed by true artists, with a genuine feeling for what is required in drapery, and the material was probably richer and more substantial than that of the present day. Our designers, like the French, seem to imagine that the whole pattern is to be exhibited distended, like a piece of tambour-work upon a frame, instead of being broken up and half-concealed in the natural folds of the drapery. To a certain extent they were justified during the supremacy of crinoline, but we are happily escaping from that thralldom, and now, perhaps, our textile artists will come to understand that patterns in a dress are not pictures, and design them with regard chiefly to their effect in producing a pleasing play of line in the drapery, and a harmonious arrangement of color.

Materials and patterns require to be selected with reference to the figure of the wearer. What would assume an air of distinction upon a tall and stately person, would not be becoming to a brisk, mercurial little maiden, the living embodiment of perpetual motion, nor to the figure of a short, stout matron.

So again, the dress that would be beautiful and graceful when falling in long, free folds, accommodating themselves to the natural motions of the form, would be utterly ruined by straining over crinoline, or being cut into flounces, puffs, or ruffing.

It should also be remembered, in adapting colors and materials to the figure, that they have as much effect there as upon the complexion or hair. The heavy, rich materials which suit a tall figure, look awkward upon a small person, and while all dark colors impart an appearance of slender proportions, light ones will certainly render conspicuous any tendency to corpulence. Full, light drapery should be worn only by those of slender figure, while those who are too short must be content with dark colors, and tightly-fitting garments.

HOW TO MAKE A DRESS.

To make a dress handsomely, well-fitting, and perfect in every respect, is so important an addition to the art of dressing well, that this chapter needs no apology for its insertion. It is one of the advantages that women possess over the stronger sex, that they can, in an emergency, dispense with the assistance of the milliner, dressmaker, and seamstress. In such emergencies it is no small advantage to a lady to be able to cut and make a dress, although some experience and skill are necessary for a perfect success.

The first rule for dressmaking is to have all the materials required ready before the sewing is commenced ; the sewing-silk should be neatly wound, the body-lining ready, hooks and eyes, stiff facing-muslin, sleeve-linings, skirt-lining, cord, trimming, buttons, whalebones, skirt-braid, cotton, wadding, and all requisite sewing implements at hand.

Measure off first the breadths of the skirt, being careful to allow a strong turning top and bottom. Then pin or tack the breadths together, and, if gored, be careful that the gores are even, and the sweep of the skirt falls exactly in the center of the back breadth. Be careful that no breadth is turned wrong side out, or with the pattern upside down. You must allow in the gored skirt for the stretching of the cut edge more than the selvage, or the work will pucker.

In a plain skirt, begin your run at the bottom, that any unevenness may come at the top, but in a gored skirt you must begin at the top, and let the difference, if any, come at the bottom. In case of a cut edge and a selvage coming together, however, the selvage must be held uppermost, and notched here and there to prevent puckers.

As a gored skirt hangs lower in the center of the breadths than on the edges, the first turning of the hem must allow for that difference, and be laid deeper where it would otherwise droop. It is also necessary to baste the turning of a gored skirt carefully, and also to baste down the facing, as it will be likely to stretch at the top of the hem or facing. The fullness at the top must be held in evenly, or it will make an awkward fold at the seams.

It is important to make all the fastenings of a dress very secure, as there is generally a severe strain upon all of them. The pocket-hole, placket, arm-holes, waist-binding, every part, indeed, must be firmly and neatly secured against danger of ripping. It is a sure sign of slovenly dressmaking when the sleeves rip from the arm-holes, or a pocket falls out after any unusual weight being placed in it.

After the skirt is cut and basted, the sleeves are the next part to cut. It is necessary to have a paper pattern exactly as you wish to cut the sleeve; double the lining, and cut it accurately by this pattern, leaving a half inch all round for seams. It is better always to cut the lining double, as you thus cut both sleeves at once, and avoid all danger of getting one larger than the other. Next double the material of the dress, and cut it by the lining, laying the selvage to the straight length of the pattern.

When skirt and sleeves are cut, the most difficult part of the dressmaking must be undertaken, namely, to get an accurately fitted waist. Take a piece of thin but strong paper, and fold one corner the length of the front, pinning it to the corset. Spread the paper very smoothly across the bust to the shoulder, and fold it to fit the figure exactly; cut away round the arm, and draw it smoothly under it, then cut again to the waist, allowing fullness enough for darts and the width of the seams. Another piece of paper must now be pinned to the back, and fitted to meet the front. This being half the body, you have only to fold the lining so as to cut each back double, to get the back and each front for the front. In cutting the material, however, it is best to baste the lining down, and be careful to allow for the hems on each side of the front. It is generally preferable to cut away the darts, but if very narrow they may be left.

The back will generally fit better if side-bodies are put in, instead of cutting it all in one piece. As soon as the whole is cut, baste it together and try it on, wrong side outward, pinning the seams, the darts, and the side-bodies to fit the figure, and altering the bastings to suit the measurement.

Having cut and basted your dress, the next step is to put in neatly together. First run the breadths of the skirt, making it full or narrow, short or long, according to the fashion. Rut the seams very evenly, pinning the end to a stationary pin-cushion to prevent puckering. If the skirt is lined, it will hang better if the lining is the same width as the material, and run in with it at each breadth. Cut even at the top and bottom, and whip thickly. Next put on the facing, if the skirt is not lined, or, if lined, put on the stiff facing at the bottom, and hem to the lining, being careful that no stitches show through on the right side; if not lined, the facing had better be notched at the top, and run down. Be careful in running your seams to leave the space for the pocket and the placket slit. Hem the latter, and lay the upper hem over the lower, stitching it firmly at the bottom. Next put on the skirt braid and put in the pocket. If you trim with flounces, cut them always crosswise of the material, or they will not hang gracefully. Each breadth must be halved and quartered. Run in a strong cord at the top, and divide the fullness evenly before drawing the cord, and stitching the flounce down. If you wish a ruffle above the cord, run it into a tape casing, as much below the top as you wish the width of the ruffle. Box-plaits, ruffles, indeed all kinds of trimming made of the material, must be carefully measured and cut out before the skirt is put together. If trimming of different material is used, the prevailing fashion must govern the choice and manner of putting it on.

The sleeves must be made next. If there are two seams, run a cord along the upper one, covered with the material, and sew down on the outside. Cord at the wrist, and turn the lining inside to conceal the seam. Stitch the long seams together, lining and material at the same time, if it is practicable. Always trim the sleeves before putting them into the arm-hole, and, where it can be done, before stitching up the inside seam.

Next, stitch together the waist as it is basted, putting a covered cord round the arm-holes, and on the neck and waist. Even if a band is put at the throat, and a belt at the waist, they will appear neater and stronger if they are properly corded.

The skirt is next to be put on the waist, being first gathered, plaited, or sloped, according to its fashion. If there are two skirts, put the lower one on the waist-band, and the other on a belt of the material, strongly lined.

If a sacque or cape is made, it should be cut out with the dress, basted and fitted. A cape should be cut from a paper pattern, and lined with some light muslin, a little stiff. A cord should be stitched round the edge, with the lining, and the latter then turned and pressed to conceal the seam. This is not necessary if the cape is to be trimmed at the edge, when the material must be cut large enough to hem down on the lining. A sacque may be corded, hemmed, or bound, according to the trimming. Sleeveless sacques must be neatly corded round the arm-holes.

These directions are given principally for woolen or silk dresses, and for a plain waist and separate skirt. The dress made all in one must be cut from a paper pattern, and will be so difficult an undertaking that the inexperienced dressmaker could scarcely succeed from any written directions.

Thin materials for evening dresses should be lined with silk, and the waist made with some fullness, corded in round the shoulders and at the waist; the sleeves will be prettier puffed.

Cotton prints for summer wear are not always lined; but should be protected under the arms and round the arm-holes by a narrow lining of cotton. Lawns, barèges, organdies, indeed all summer fabrics will wear better, be more easily washed and ironed, and look better, if the lining is made entirely separate from the dress. A handsomely trimmed corset cover, sewed to a tucked cambric skirt, makes a pretty lining for a thin dress. Thin fabrics are prettier faced with book-muslin than they are hemmed, excepting plain materials which can be hemmed. Figured goods show the irregularity of the pattern very badly in a hem.

ARRANGEMENT OF COLORS.

It has been said that it is essential to harmony of effect that the colors in combination should bear not only a due relation, but also a proper proportion to one another. But it is impossible to assign the relative quantities that will produce the most perfect harmony. If such directions could be given they would be as numerous as the combinations. But harmony of color will not admit of a quantative analysis. What are the proper proportions is very much a matter of perception and feeling. We might say with tolerable certainty that colors or tones of equal intensity should never be brought together in equal quantities, and other general rules might also be proposed, but they would be found to resolve themselves into deductions from the principles with which we have been dealing, and will, in substance, if not in words, occur to all who give to the subject a moderate amount of attention.

Happily in dress equal quantities are hardly practicable. The nearest approach to danger is from the contiguity of cloak, shawl, sacque or other upper garment.

The most convenient way of illustrating the relations of colors, and indicating the bearings of the principles of harmony and contrast in the combination and arrangement of colors in dress, will be to take some of the leading colors and their modifications, and point out what other colors agree or disagree with them. As the easiest mode of classifying the colors for our purpose, we will take the primaries first, putting under each its leading modification; then the secondaries, the neutrals, and so on.

Uncertainty and misapprehension frequently occur in speaking of colors from the indefinite and often different ideas people attach to the words red, blue, green, and the like. In large and expensive works precision can, to a certain extent, be secured by giving colored scales and diagrams. But even these are imperfect and often unsatisfactory. Another method, first proposed by Moses Harris, in the last century, is that of referring the color to some common flower, mineral, or other natural object. This plan, which has also been adopted by Sir Gardner Wilkinson in his work "On Color," a work to which we are indebted for some of the suggestions in the annexed summary, we shall follow wherever it seems necessary to distinguish a distinct color from one of its varieties.

In this summary it will be understood that the color which stands at the head of the paragraph is the principal color of a dress, those named afterwards being the subsidiary colors, either employed in smaller quantities, or as trimmings, to relieve, brighten, heighten, or in any way modify it. Discretion and judgment in the wearer must decide much of the quantity desirable to be used.

RED (*Field Poppy, Verbena Melindris*).

Red is a color seldom used for dress, but it is the parent of numerous varieties, and may serve as a subsidiary color, though seldom as effective as scarlet in ribbons or trimmings. The complementary of red, a pale green, looks well with it, in small quantities, but a pale sea-green *celadon*, a pearl or silver-gray, looks better.

Scarlet, in an opera-cloak or fancy dress, has a brilliant effect trimmed with gold, and harmonizes well with white. In ribbons or velvet trimmings it is a valuable addition to gray or drab, or to any of the light neutral tints. Will bear black lace or swan's down.

Crimson (*Cactus Speciocissimus*) is often seen with blue in paintings, but it requires white to harmonize. Crimson will also bear blue and gold, or orange, but they must be combined with discrimination; it will bear orange alone, but is improved by the softening of black or white lace. Crimson and purple are discordant alone, but crimson will bear purple

and pale green in very small quantities. Crimson is dangerous to the complexion, unless very clear, or glowing and
slightly olive, when white should be placed between the complexion and the color.

Claret has a little purple in its composition. Harmonizes
with orange and gold, but not with yellow. Very rich in effect trimmed with black lace, of which it will bear a large
quantity.

Magenta may be regarded as a variety of claret. It is improved by contact with black, injured by green, destroys scarlet placed upon it in small quantities.

Maroon has a tendency to brown. Harmonizes with gold
or orange. Will bear a very little green. Heightened in
effect by white or black. Loses brilliancy in gas-light. Is
apt to bring out the green in the complexion, unless relieved
by a decided green in the hair-ribbon or neck-tie. A color
that suits but few, and requires skillful handling,

Pink is suitable only for very young ladies. Looks best
alone, or with pure white. Is effective with narrow lines of
black, or black lace. A good color for evening wear, as it
lights up well in artificial light; bears silver trimming well.

Cerise harmonizes well with silver-gray, lilac, or a pale
lavender; will bear, in addition, a few sprigs of gold, and
then may allow a point of scarlet or crimson. Blue with
cerise is very harsh; but blue and gold, deftly arranged in
small quantities, will haamonize with it.

BLUE (*Lapis-lazuli or Corn-flower*).

Harmonizes with its complementary, orange. Discordant
with yellow. Intolerable with green—although in nature
blue flowers look beautiful nestled in green leaves. Blue and
a warm, rich brown, not too dark (the color of the horse-
chestnut), harmonize well, or a little white may be added.
Blue requires white next the complexion. Other harmonious
combinations are: blue, crimson, and gold, or orange. The
same with purple, very effective in patterns, if lines of black
are used to prevent the too sharp contact of the contrasting
colors, and in occasional spots. In the same way a rich
brown, scarlet, or crimson and gold may be made to harmonize, with blue as the principal color.

Light-blue is only suitable for daylight. As an evening dress
it is ineffective, the artificial light changing it to an unpleas-
ant light-green. Looks well alone, or with velvet trimmings
of the same color. White agrees with it, even in large quantity; black can be used only very sparingly, and only in lace.
Drab. or a diffused gray, with a point of red, admissible upon
light-blue, but very trying to most complexions.

YELLOW (*Furze-blossom, Buttercups*).

Pure yellow is not much used for dress, orange on the one
side, straw or amber on the other, being much richer, and
more agreeable to the eye. It harmonizes best with its complementary, purple. Black is also of great value as a trimming, and may be used freely.

Amber, Straw, Primrose and *Canary*, are feebler in effect
than orange. These shades are rendered still weaker by contact with any strong color or tone. Of these, however, purple
is the best. Black looks well in lace only. Trimmings of a
faint crimson or cerise have a pretty and cheerful effect, but
require a little dash in the wearer. White may be used as
lace, but with care, and will call for the addition of small
points of stronger color.

ORANGE (*Common Garden Marigold, or the Orange Fruit*).

Is very effective in the evening, when Fashion permits its
adoption. Orange satin with purple has a splendid appearance, but suits only a tall, commanding figure. Black, especially in lace, is an efficient contrast. White is less effective, but looks well by gas or candle-light. Orange is the
complementary of, and harmonizes well with blue, but they
would form a doubtful combination in dress; minute points of
scarlet, black, or white, might be added, but for dress orange
is best alone or with purple, black, or white. Suits brunette
complexions, and will bear a rich crimson in the hair, especially if the dress is subdued in tone by a profusion of black
lace.

GREEN (*Grass — inclining neither to blue nor yellow — Emerald*).

Is very grateful to the eye, but a difficult color to manage
in a dress. All the varieties of green are affected, and a few
improved by artificial light. Harmonizes, but not agreeably,
with its complementary, a pale red; better with pale scarlet;
but for an evening dress is most effective with gold, either
bright or dull. In the open air agrees well with white, and
may be relieved with scarlet or crimson, used very sparingly
and judiciously. Is dulled in effect by black.

Light green looks well with white. May be used with
small points of a rich brown, or trimmed with a darker shade
of the same color, but is an unmanageable color, and very
trying to the complexion.

Dark green. Titian has clothed the figures in some of his
most famous pictures in a very deep green, but he has taken
care to bring large quantities of white against the complex-

ion, and generally has a bright crimson near, to balance the composition. It looks well with the glowing Venetian complexion, but should be used with care, as but few complexions will bear the contact well.

PURPLE (*Nightshade-blossom, Amethyst, Plum*).

The regal color has a magnificent effect with gold. Purple silk may be trimmed with orange. A clear crimson, or, better, scarlet brightens it, but requires management as to quantity; this combination is improved by gold, or a little orange, or amber. A very minute quantity of green, as a tiny sprig, suits some shades. White and black may be used freely. Purple is most effective in rich material, as velvet, heavy silks, poplins, or merinoes, and loses effect in thin goods.

Puce requires gold or orange. Is brightened by scarlet. Not a good color, and very trying to most complexions.

Lilac, Lavender, Mauve, harmonize with cerise, used sparingly, and with gold, but are better trimmed with the same color of a shade slightly darker or lighter. White may be used freely, black rather sparingly. Lavender takes black for half-mourning; mauve takes white or black for slight mourning.

GRAY.

The grays, like all the neutral colors, are very valuable for quiet dresses, and adapt themselves well to different forms. They make a dress of simple elegance with trimmings of the same color, black or white, yet serve admirably as a ground for any of the bright colors. Crimson or scarlet is most effective upon a gray ground. The grays require white next the complexion when trimmed with their own color. They are very effective with a very small point of intense color.

DRAB.

The *drabs, fawn, mode,* and *mouse colors* have much the same general character as the grays, but are not so cold and severe in tone. Crimson, blue, and green in the neck-ribbon or head-dress relieve any of these colors, and they will all bear bright-colored trimmings. Walking-dresses are effective in any of these, but they are equally suitable for indoor dresses, and, like grays, adapt themselves readily to a quiet, elegant, or rich style.

BLACK,

When not worn for mourning, will bear the bright colors for trimming or ornament, and sets off gold ornaments effectively White relieves it very happily, and it is the best background in velvet for diamonds. To some complexions it is always becoming, but becomes gloomy by constant wear. Is very effective in lace worn over bright-colored silks or white satin.

WHITE.

White muslin is especially appropriate for the young and for festive occasions. Is suggestive of pleasant memories and associations; admits of the gayest and brightest trimmings, though scarlet and blue are most effective. With white silks for evening wear and occasions of ceremony, a heavier style of trimming is necessary. Dull gold is very effective with rich white silk or satin. Lace of either white or black looks well, and colored tulle is effective over a white silk or satin underdress, as is also colored silk under white tulle, lace, or tarlatan, for young people. Faintly tinted whites are effective with the color of the tint as trimming, but look badly in contact with pure white.

We have thus run over the leading colors, and indicated the manner in which they may be treated in accordance with the laws of color. Our cursory remarks make no pretense to be in any way exhaustive. They are offered only as suggestions. Some of them, we are fully äware, will be found out of the usual course. Try these cautiously—most of them will be found safe, as they are directed by sound principle. All of them will be found useful as hints for the foundation of a dress where skill and judgment will dictate the details.

COLOR IN RELATION TO COMPLEXION, HAIR, &c.

IN the last chapter we noticed the leading colors and their treatment in dress, but only incidentally alluded to their appropriateness, or otherwise to personal peculiarities. Yet it needs but little observation to be satisfied that a color or arrangement of colors, graceful and becoming upon one lady, would be quite unsuited to another, although each may be beautiful and attractive. A lady's skill and taste in dress are, perhaps, shown in nothing so clearly as in selecting and arranging colors to suit her individuality of character and appearance. Little guidance is possible in the former respect. A lady of grave habits will instinctively avoid a glaring, or even a light, fanciful style of dress. A gay girl will allow her fancy more play, and shrink from the somber hues and grave fashions, while the retiring, quiet lady will adopt a still different style. The young bride will appear to charming advantage in what would be simply absurd upon the matron advanced in years; while, on the other hand, we do not wish to see the young maiden arrayed in the colors and fabrics becoming to her grandmother,

With reference to appearance, however, something more may be said. All who have touched upon the subject have given some directions for the selection or arrangement of colors according to the complexion, color of the hair and eyes, and general character of the wearer's beauty. Many of the directions are of comparatively little value, deductions from a theory of colors requiring, however correct in themselves, to be modified in individual cases to an extent which the student of color in the abstract can scarcely be expected to appreciate.

There is one source of error incident to all the results derived from theoretical considerations when applied to dress, which it may be useful to point out.

The rules for producing harmony and contrast are based upon results observed in looking at selected colors placed side by side, or allowing the eye to rest upon a particular color, till, on removing it, the complementary is seen. But in dress, and especially in considering its color in connection with the hair and complexion, it must be borne in mind that the influence of the one on the other is not simultaneous. It is something very different from that produced by two strips of color side by side, or by colors seen at the same moment—as in a flower or the wing of a butterfly. The action, whatever it is, is successive. The eye, resting on the dress, is filled by its color, and then rests upon the face of the wearer, or the contrary. It is an alternate, and not a simultaneous effect that is produced. Thus, the eye after resting for a time upon a blue dress, will be susceptible of the complementary, orange, and insensible for the moment to blue. No lady, then, should wonder if her blue eyes were less effective when she wore a bright blue dress, and a yellow dress would utterly destroy the effect of bright blonde hair, or hair of the reddish-gold would ill bear knots of orange ribbons.

These are trite illustrations, but will better serve the purpose of enforcing the fact so important in connection with this section of the subject, that the influence of the color of the dress upon the complexion is due, not to the simultaneous, but to the successive action upon the retina.

The eye, filled with the color of the dress, is rendered thus particularly susceptible to rays of an opposite color, and being moved, whilst in that condition, to the face, colors or hues of the color last looked upon are lost or depreciated, whilst those of the opposite kind have an increased value. This is the secret of the heightening or lowering of all weak colors by the proximity of larger masses and stronger colors.

But remember it is not best to trust entirely to any stated

rules, however sound and plausible they may be in theory. Ovid's advice in this matter will always be the safest:

"No complexion can bear every hue; try them all; wear that which best becomes you."

Complexions require the colors that enforce their peculiar excellence, and render their defects less conspicuous.

Blue suits the blonde complexion, but is trying to blue or bluish-gray eyes, and while it enriches golden hair, is liable to exaggerate any tinge of yellow in the complexion. How then is a lady to reconcile these conditions? White should separate the blue from direct contact with the complexion, and then a bright golden brooch or chain will keep down any slightly yellow hue in the throat as the hair will subdue that in the face. The eyes, if they have any life, flash, or sparkle, will take care of themselves.

In the same way intensely pallid complexions, especially if shaded still further by black hair, will not bear a dead white against the face, and only the softest and finest lace in collar or ruffle is becoming.

The way to lower any tint that is excessive in the face is to bring a strong color of the same class in close proximity to it; but it is not always a desirable remedy, and it is only necessary to resort to it when the dress is not quite suited to the complexion.

Pink, as was said before, is only fitted for the young. It is a charming color, and those to whom it is suited look very graceful in it. The pale, sickly, and those of an olive hue, had better avoid it.

White is similar in its conditions. It beautifies and sets off to perfection a healthy young face, but deepens the gloom of a sad or sickly one.

A florid complexion is rendered more florid by green. To take an extreme illustration, if a lady were so unfortunate as to be the possessor of a red nose, her keenest rival could not desire for her any worse fate than that on some momentous occasion she should wear a green dress. On the other hand, an excess of red may be counteracted by a judicious arrangement of crimson in the dress, or near the face. But this must be used cautiously, or the effect may be ludicrously opposite to that intended. Red will not always cure, but sometimes seems to deepen the same hue in the face, a result, however, it will be found, if the case be analyzed, of the presence of other elements beside the red in the complexion.

Black seldom agrees with a very florid complexion, and requires white with a very pallid one. It will, however, suit a fair and ruddy face better than a dark, ruddy one.

Brunettes look most brilliant in an orange dress, or in

orange and purple, or orange and black. Red, a deep pink, or crimson, in the form of flowers, ribbons, or trimmings, may be valuable to clear up other colors, or to act as a point or focus. Scarlet is more dangerous, and should be well tested before it is used. Blue is always inimical to the brunette; if used at all, it should be of a deep, rich shade, well toned with black lace, and relieved by deep crimson in the hair. Light blue is almost invariably unbecoming. When the face is decidedly dark strong dark colors will have the effect of rendering it lighter by contrast. A deep purple is sometimes of value—dependent, of course, on the special half-tones of the face—but it will require light and bright subsidiary colors as trimmings or ornaments. If the face be dark and pallid, dark and strong colors should be used cautiously and sparingly.

Titian constantly brings white into contact with the deep, glowing, healthy complexions he delighted to paint, and then has, either as the principal drapery, or close at hand, the richest crimson in considerable quantity. But this would be too decided for the delicacy of most American complexions, which would hardly sustain such splendor. Our brunettes, and even those whose complexions approach an olive, must be content with more sober harmonies. But the principle is there. There are complexions which require deep, rich tones and colors, with points of decided contrast. Maroon is apt to bring out any latent green in the complexion, and therefore should be used but seldom in direct contact with it. The interposition of white is sometimes sufficient to counteract this tendency. If insufficient, emeralds or other green stones may be used.

A light, rosy complexion harmonizes admirably with a silver-gray or pearl. The gray tints, however, will be found to suit most complexions, partly because they form so good a ground for any strong color that may be required by the character of the complexion or the color of the hair, but also because from their variety it is comparatively easy to find a suitable tone for almost every style of personal appearance. But the suitable tone is important. We have just said, for instance, that a silver or pearl gray harmonizes with a clear, light, rosy complexion, but such a gray would inevitably reveal any lurking sallowness in the skin, and be found to deepen any dusky hue, or increase any dullness in the face.

A pale complexion, if healthy and natural, is improved by black, but, as remarked before, black does not suit the extremely pallid, the sickly complexion, or the pallid and dark. If employed by them, the accessories must be skillfully adjusted.

Ristori is a finished artist in dress as well as in acting, and those who have seen her may object here that she never looks more magnificent than when robed in black, although usually pallid and dark. But it is to be remembered that she is seen upon the stage at such a distance that the eye takes in her whole figure and face at a glance. Dress and face are stamped on the retina simultaneously; and further, from the distance, and the strong and peculiar light under which she is seen, however pale she may appear, darkness and sallowness of hue are lost sight of entirely in the general effect. It is the tender gradations and delicate half-tints seen close at hand which are most affected for beauty or the reverse by neighboring colors.

Enough has probably been said by way of *hints* on the management of colors in connection with the complexion. The reader will have no difficulty in pursuing the subject to any desirable extent. One or two general remarks may, however, be added. In considering the effect of contiguous colors on the complexion, it will be necessary to observe whether it is produced by contrast, or whether any part of the effect results from reflection. With the bonnets formerly worn this was an essential consideration. Now so little of the bonnet is seen from the front view, that their influence upon the hair is more important than the effect upon the complexion. Flowers and other ornaments play a much more important part, but their influence is due to contiguity, to their contrast with, or action upon, the prevailing hue, the half-tints and latent shades of the complexion, and to reflection, in but few instances.

Colors favorable to the complexion are not always at the same time favorable to the hair, but here flowers or other ornaments will usually supply the remedy.

Black hair has its depth and brilliancy emphasized by a scarlet, white, or orange flower ; but a dull red near it tends to render it dull and brownish by imparting a portion of its own hue; this is a well-known effect of some colors, in certain connections, on others in immediate contact with them. Glossy black hair has a superb effect when decorated with diamond sprays, and bears well ornaments of lusterless gold, and pearls.

Light brown hair bears well the contact of blue, which brings out effectively the golden tint.

Dark brown hair will also bear light blue in quantity, or a deeper blue in smaller proportion. If it is a little dull, lacking gloss and liveliness, a pale yellowish-green will be found becoming.

Pure golden hair is a rare tint. It will bear blue best, but is also effective with pearls and delicate white flowers.

Auburn hair, if too much inclined to red, will be improved by close contact with scarlet. The golden-red will be enhanced by a blue flower, pale green leaves, or a band of black. Purple will also serve to bring out the reddish-golden tints.

Flaxen hair is difficult to manage. Purple is becoming to some tints; blue will bring out the golden tints, but is dangerous if there is a tendency to the tallow hue.

Before quitting this section, it should be observed that even in the choice of color for ornaments very much depends upon the manner of arranging the hair. When the hair is flowing in loose curls beside the face, there is such a constantly varying play of light and answering shadow, the color of the hair itself is so modified by the light which falls upon it, that little more in the way of color or ornament is required. The present fashions, however, for dressing the hair, allow of more opportunity for the display of artistic taste and contrivance, and adapt themselves well to many styles of beauty.

To the sunny, cheerful face of the youthful maiden there can be no elaborate style of *coiffure* so becoming as the free, natural flow of hair in curling or waving masses, or even in the broad braids of a few years back, yet there is a certain dignity imparted to some countenances by the present contrivances of the Parisian hair-dressers.

The point for us to note, however, is that all the new styles of dressing the hair admit, and in many cases require, artificial additions, and that with one or the other of them, therefore, there can be no want of opportunity to introduce color to any desired extent.

The color of the tiny bonnets now in vogue, as we have already observed, has more influence upon the hair than upon the complexion; and the same may be said of the smart little hats which very young ladies affect so much. But the fashions change so rapidly in this respect, that it is not worth while to dwell upon them here at any length.

JEWELRY.

JEWELS may be made to serve more purposes, even as ornaments, than would be supposed by those who have never given the subject much attention. They possess not merely their own intrinsic value, or a value as advertising the wealth of the possessor, but independent of these considerations, they have an artistic value and use.

It has been shown of what great service gold might be made in harmonizing contrasting colors, and in adding splendor to even the richest. In many other cases its value is of no less importance in subduing colors which are harsh, crude, or undesirably strong.

The watch-chain and bosom-pin may in such cases be turned to excellent account, but judgment must be exercised in their application. Dead, or lusterless gold, and bright, or burnished, should be selected for the purpose not indifferently, but according to the effect they are desired to produce.

In the selection of necklaces and bracelets, the texture and color of the neck and arm should influence the choice not only of the golden ones, but of the enameled, and those encrusted with gems. The same remarks that apply to the effect of colors upon the complexion will be found valuable for reference in choosing necklace and bracelets, the snowy white, round arm, or polished ivory throat, bearing the contact of gems that would render an arm or neck inclined to sallowness, or tinged too much with red, simply hideous. On the other hand, these latent tints of yellow, green, or red, may be in a great measure subdued and concealed by skillful adjustment of the strong points of color in the ornaments upon their surface.

Gems are a valuable addition to dress, as points of intense color to serve as the focus or concentration of some diffused or scattered color, or as a point of condensed and brilliant contrast. As a contrast, a brilliant gem resting upon a dark, rich color, black, or pure white, is of singular value.

But it is not alone as points of intense tone, of sharp, brilliant contrast that they are available. They serve also as suggestive of that similitude in dissimilitude of which poets and poetic commentators have often spoken. Of course we must not rate their value too high. Steele writes:

"What jewel can the charming Cleora place in her ears that can please the beholder so much as her eyes? The cluster of diamonds can add no beauty to the fair chest of ivory that supports it."

And again he says:

"The pearl necklace can only be of use to attract the eye of the beholder, and turn it from the imperfections of the features and shape."

But it must be borne in mind that Steele was writing in the character of a censor, and his object was to set bounds to a prevalent extravagance. A diamond cluster will enhance the brilliancy of the whitest skin, and pearls are the most perfect adornment for a lovely neck. Yet these are also dangerous additions to the sallow and over-florid complexions.

To be really effective, jewelry should be employed sparingly, and with discrimination. Better far a little that is really valuable and well-selected, than a profusion of cheap, ill-assorted ornaments, though it may be bad and in bad taste if it is ever so costly.

What a lady requires is to have sufficient for choice, as what will be effective and beautiful with one dress may entirely ruin the appearance of another of different style and color. Pure gold is valuable with almost any dress, but the gems require more discretion in their use.

The proper selection and use of jewelry is a prime test of good or bad taste. Especially should ladies seek to possess artistic jewelry, even if they find it difficult to obtain. The superiority of beautiful designs and forms over mere lavish employment of material is shown in the exquisite Greek, Etruscan and Roman designs which can now be obtained, and which certainly ought to entirely supersede the clumsier patterns so long in vogue.

Jewels of perfect forms set in the elaborate and exquisitely beautiful designs of Cellini and Holbein would add grace to the loveliest forms and fairest complexions.

Stones, however rich and rare in themselves, can be proved of secondary importance where the designs are artistic and perfect. Enamel with spots of gold, a few brilliants, emeralds, rubies, or pearls, disposed with taste and intelligence, can be made to produce all the effect that can be desired, even in point of color, while delicate workmanship and chasteness of design will far out-balance a more valuable collection of stones in a ruder setting.

OCCASION.

Having fully considered the subject of color in relation to dress in the preceding chapters, we now come to another consideration of equal importance in the eyes of those who are anxious to acquire the art of dressing well. This is the style, texture and general effect of dress in relation to the occasion upon which it is to be worn.

No lady requires to be told that it would be inappropriate to go to church in her ball-dress, or to appear at the opera in her chintz wrapper, but there are many nicer shades of discrimination which will sometimes puzzle even those who consider the subject of paramount importance.

A toilet may be offensive to good taste by being out of place or out of season, as well as by being glaringly inharmonious in color or slovenly in detail. The idea that you may escape unnoticed, that "just for once" you may appear inconsistently dressed, is a dangerous one, and apt to draw upon the wearer the credit for eccentricity, or bad taste, which a true lady should carefully avoid.

In suiting a dress to the occasion upon which it is to be worn, there is more to be considered than the mere personal appearance of the wearer. In itself the dress may be exquisitely tasteful, graceful, and becoming to both face and figure, and yet, from its want of adaptiveness to the occasion upon which it is worn, will appear absurd and most unbecoming.

It is also, when accepting invitations, due to your host or hostess to dress in accordance with the entertainment to which you are invited. An appropriate dress will increase your popularity in society, as well as an appropriate deportment.

There is more importance than is usually attached to one occasion, and that is the dress appropriate for visits of condolence. It is not, of course, expected that you will put on mourning for your acquaintances and friends, or their relations, but in calling upon the survivors in their affliction, it may affect them painfully, and impress them with a want of sympathy on your part, if you appear in very bright or gay colors. A quiet style of dress, although it may in itself pass unnoticed, will not jar painfully upon hearts recently bereaved, and it is as delicate a way of expressing sympathy as is a quiet tone of conversation, or the avoidance of frivolous subjects.

And in connection with this subject it must be remembered that every part of the dress must be considered in reference to occasion. The out-door costume must have bonnet or hat, cloak or shawl, gloves, boots, and other details adapted to the festival or party as well as the dress. A dress for a sailing-party, if perfect in all other respects, would be ruined by an expensive lace shawl, or a pair of delicate, thin-soled boots. So, in an in-door dress, heavy walking-boots would be as inappropriate as a bonnet or parasol.

Fashion is such a capricious goddess that it would be impossible to follow all her whims and vagaries in our little volume; we do not propose to give the fashionable costume for every occasion, but to lay down such general rules as will enable our readers to appear appropriately dressed for all occasions, if they but add to them the prevailing mode of trimming and style.

MORNING DRESSES—BREAKFAST.

MORNING dresses must be in a manner adapted to the circumstances of the wearer, as well as the hour of the day. A

lady in her own home at breakfast may wear a simpler costume than would be suitable if visiting, or at the table of a
large boarding-house or hotel.

If the wearer expects to pass a portion of the morning in
domestic duties, the care of an infant, the dressing of older
children for school, the preparation of delicacies for the table,
or arranging her own parlor or bedroom, the most suitable
dress is a chintz or gingham, made loosely enough to allow
free play of the figure. A linen collar and cuffs form a suitable finish, and the hair should be neatly arranged without
ornament, unless the loss of hair compels the use of a plain
cap. The dress for receiving morning calls will be given in
another chapter.

It is well, over the simple dress described, to wear a large
gingham apron while engaged in domestic pursuits, as it will
protect the dress, and can be more easily washed.

For breakfast in visiting, or at a public table, the loose dress
of home would be out of place. A wrapper is suitable only
for an invalid, or the dressing-room, and the breakfast dress
should fit the waist closely, even if allowed to remain open in
the skirt over a dressy petticoat. French cambric, white
barred muslin, piqué, or Marseilles, and even lawn, are all
perfectly suitable materials for summer breakfast dresses, and
should be trimmed tastefully, as the prevailing fashion dictates. In winter any woolen goods made simply and trimmed
quietly will make an appropriate breakfast dress.

It is permitted to wear a gayer style of cashmere and delaine
in a breakfast dress than in the material for occasions later in
the day, but these will be found more becoming if trimmed
with folds of silk of a solid color, especially broad folds down
the front.

Breakfast caps must be light, but not very dressy, and be
careful that the hair is neatly arranged under them. No cap,
however graceful, will compensate for slovenly, rough locks,
guiltless of comb and brush, and scarcely half hidden beneath
it.

Linen is the most suitable material for the collar and cuffs
worn at breakfast, though narrow ruffles of lace may be sub-
stituted. The more expensive laces are as much out of place
as a head-dress of artificial flowers would be.

Let the jewelry worn at breakfast be of the simplest de-
scription, and only such as is absolutely necessary to fasten
the collar, cuffs, or belt. Bracelets, necklaces, and other articles worn for ornament alone, are entirely out of place, and
so are expensive gems or elaborate designs.

Ribbons, unless used for actual trimming, and velvets, are
also in bad taste. There is no occasion when a severe simplicity of style is more becoming than at the breakfast-table.

The same costume in which you would appear at the table of a friend to whom you were paying a visit is also suitable for the head of your own table when you are entertaining visitors.

Slippers are always permissible in the breakfast dress, though those of embroidered cloth or canvas are in bad taste outside of the dressing-room. Kid, with a rosette or bow of ribbon, is the most dressy slipper allowable for appearance at table.

MORNING DRESSES—SHOPPING.

In dressing for a shopping expedition the lady skilled in dressing well will be observed to be studiously neat, quiet, almost what might be called business-like, in her attire. She will avoid anything decided in her appearance, or in any way dressy, while she will endeavor to have all compact, quiet, and lady-like.

The most useful dresses for shopping are composed of materials that will bear the crush of crowded stores without injury, and fringes, laces, streamers of any kind, are best avoided. Flounces are apt to suffer severely in a shopping tour, and long, trailing skirts will be apt to carry home a long rent, or the stains from the floors or articles always more or less in the way in large stores.

Jewelry is entirely out of place, and the danger of loss is very great. If the watch is worn it is best to have the chain as much concealed as possible, and occasionally to assure by touching it that it is safe. Bracelets, or showy ornaments of any kind, are in excessively bad taste, and any conspicuous article of attire is best avoided.

In shopping dresses the pocket should be deep and strong, but it is better for small packages to carry a leather satchel in the hand. A sacque, or tight-fitting coat, will be found much more serviceable than a shawl or cloak, either of which will be apt to catch and drag small articles from a counter.

Kid gloves, if worn in shopping, had best be removed from the right hand when fabrics are handled and examined, as the contact may soil, while the movement will certainly strain them badly. Lisle thread gloves in summer, and cloth ones in winter, will be found much more serviceable than kid.

As shopping is usually undertaken in the morning, the simpler the dress the more suitable it will appear. Rich silks, velvets, or any thin goods, will suffer more from one morning's shopping than from any other ordinary wear, while they are at the same time in bad taste.

Alpaca, poplin, and linen, are all serviceable for shopping, or any of the more inexpensive fabrics used for walking-dresses may be worn. Let the color be neutral and subdued, and the style of making quiet, avoiding over trimming, ruffling, or flounces. Black is not a very good dress, as it shows so soon any contact with the dust unavoidably encountered. Linen collar and cuffs are most suitable, and strong walking-boots will be found the best.

The bonnet or hat should be of quiet color and inexpensive material, avoiding feathers, gay flowers, or long streamers. In stormy weather the waterproof suit, with hood drawn over the head, will be more convenient than an umbrella, which is very much in the way, and apt to be lost by carelessness or dishonesty.

If a large sum of money is carried, it is best to have two pocket-books, one to carry in the hand for change, the other carried in the bosom, or in a pocket in the skirt under the dress. A large pocket-book for change will be found convenient if you wish to procure cards from any of the dealers you may visit.

MORNING DRESSES—PROMENADE.

When the morning walk assumes the character of the promenade, where it is for pleasure rather than in the performance of a part of the duties of the day, more of richness and stylishness is not only allowable, but is to be desired.

The present fashions—1882—admit a brilliancy of coloring in the dress, and a costliness in the material, that a few years ago would have been considered glaring and in bad taste. Of course much must depend upon the age and circumstances, but color is so pleasing to many, that the gay panorama of the streets in our leading cities will doubtless be attractive to many, besides allowing scope for the display of wealth, and discrimination in the assortment of color.

Certainly ladies would confer a favor upon their fellow-citizens by venturing, as far as good taste will allow, in selecting cheerful and becoming walking-dresses. But they must be such as are pleasing in themselves, and harmoniously combined. Crude and discordant combinations or colors, that are harsh and glaring separately, are worse than the dullest hues, and suggestive of vulgar taste in the wearer. But rich and strong colors, if agreeable in themselves, and arranged with skill, may be worn without suspicion of ostentation, singularity, or a desire to attract attention, and, indeed, with the fullest recognition of modesty and taste.

In planning the arrangement of colors for a walking-dress, it must be kept in mind that the whole dress is seen, and seen at once—a contingency that seldom happens indoors. Here, therefore, is full scope for the application of the laws of harmony of color. Not only the dress itself, but cloak, shawl or sacque, if the whole be not in uniform suit, bonnet or hat, gloves, parasol, all that is worn and all that is carried will assist or impair the general effect, and none of them can be safely overlooked or neglected. The appearance of many a lady's dress is ruined, and she herself judged guilty of bad taste, by a pair of ill-chosen gloves, or a flower or feather incongruous with the rest of her apparel.

In the selection of the different articles of attire which form the walking-dress, you must bear in mind what was said in our early chapters respecting quantity and proportion. There must be no contest as to equality in the colors; no approach even to parity between the masses of color in the skirt of the robe and the cloak or sacque, if the dress is not in suit, and the difference should be greater in proportion to the distinction between the colors. One must unmistakably predominate.

This end, however, may be easily attained. Remember if there are two leading colors, both must not be primary, and if the extent of each leading color be at all nearly equal, both should not be decided colors, nor both of equal depth of tone.

For example, whether the colors contrast or are complementary, they must be opposed in intensity as well as kind. One should be decidedly darker or less vivid than the other. A vivid color, when in quantity, as in the skirt of the dress, seems to require the presence of one comparatively neutral, as in the overskirt, sacque, shawl, or cloak, in order that the contrast may be satisfactory to the eye. One less positive, or a comparatively colorless mass, will take a smaller opposing quantity of a more decided tone.

In these instances the bonnet or hat will be found very valuable in reconciling what is discordant, and supplying what is needed to complete the harmony. It will also serve to repeat, and, as a painter would say, to carry off the principal color. This principle of the repetition or distribution of the leading color is a well-known law in art. No large mass of color can safely stand alone. It should recur in smaller quantities in other parts of the dress, as it is made to recur in smaller quantities in other parts of a picture; not exactly of the same tone, nor even necessarily of the same kind, but of greater or less intensity, or as a modified tint, according to the quality and character of the principal color. But the repetitions must be judiciously managed, as to position and quantity, or the principal color will be frittered away.

The bonnet or hat must be adapted to the dress, if the dress as a whole is intended to look well. Should fashion dictate that the fronts of bonnets be again displayed, the way in which to adjust them will need care and consideration, so as to suit the shape of the face, and the chapter on complexion will be found useful in selecting becoming linings and trimmings next the face. Even now the ribbons which form the bow under the chin, or the falls of ribbon or lace on each side of the face, should be carefully selected to suit the complexion, and tested in strong daylight before being worn.

The coquettish little hats now in vogue can be made most valuable by their form and trimming towards setting off a brilliant complexion, brightening a dull one, counteracting the sallow, and subduing the over-florid tints.

The feathers, flowers, and ribbons are more serviceable in displaying the beauties of the hair by harmony or contrast, and have but little effect upon the complexion.

Collars and cuffs in the stylish walking-dress must be of fine lace, and a handsome brooch, watch-chain, ear-rings, sleeve-buttons, and bracelets (of plain gold) are admissible.

Gloves must be of kid, and the color carefully selected to harmonize with, or be in favorable contrast to the leading color in the dress.

Rich silks, velvets, and all the more expensive fabrics, are now worn in walking-dresses, and of every color. The vivid colors, however, must be deep in tone to appear well, although the neutral tints may be worn light. White is only in good taste in heavy material, such as marseilles, alpaca, and in silk can only be worn in trimmings.

However rich and stylish, the dress for promenade should never be conspicuously gay. A bright color is in much better taste as a trimming or decoration in very small quantity, than in the leading color, and the general effect is much better if subdued than if too strongly pronounced in tone, either from color or make. Dash in dress is unbecoming in the street.

In winter costumes furs will necessarily take a prominent place, and their color should be considered carefully. It is only in the richest and most elegant walking-dress that ermine can be worn, and it is really more adapted to evening than street wear. When, however, it is worn for the promenade, only velvet or the richest silk will bear the contact with its snowy surface.

On the other hand, squirrel-skin can be worn with only the most subdued dress, of plainest make and material, or in mourning.

Sables, mink, and the many varieties of brown-tinted furs, may be safely worn with almost every color, and add richness and beauty to any fabric with which they come in contact. If lined with silk, it will generally be found that a perfect match in color has a better effect than a gay-colored liniug, and the trimming will not then jar by glaring contrast with the prevailing tone of the dress.

For the country, promenade dresses may be in appearance, as well as in reality, more adapted for service than for display. Colors, fabrics, and fashions, that would be tasteful and elegant on the streets of a large city, would appear ridiculous in shaded lanes, the woods, or even the streets of a little village. Here more inexpensive fabric is in good taste, but a livelier coloring is admissible, while stouter boots, broader-brimmed hats, or warmer hoods, will be found useful and in good taste.

Over dress in the street is vulgar, but the utmost elegance and richness may be permitted if the effect is so subdued as to avoid any conspicuous display, or any glaring effect.

MORNING DRESSES,

TO RECEIVE CALLS.

THE dress for receiving morning calls will allow a lady full scope for the display of her skill in the arrangement of color to be seen by daylight.

Ladies whose visiting list is large will find it much more convenient to set aside one day in the week for the reception of morning visits, and be in their drawing-room fully ready for calls at the hour appointed.

Not only may the hostess exercise her skill and taste upon her own dress, but she has full control of the accessories. We may pity, but can scarcely forgive, the hostess who is inhuman enough to subject her callers to the test of light green wall paper, and there are other solecisms quite as bad.

The morning dress, as a rule, requires quiet colors, but, if vivid or intense tones are used, they must be controlled by the laws already given for harmony and contrast. Richness of material is admissible, and where the list of callers is very large, is requisite. Also, upon special occasions, a handsome dress is necessary, but for transient callers, the dresses appropriate for breakfast will be perfectly suitable. For New Year's calls, the richest dress is the law, and if the parlors are closed, and artificial light used, full evening dress may be worn with perfect propriety.

As a rule, quiet colors are preferable for any morning dress, but Fashion plays such strange and unexpected freaks, that it is within the bounds of possibility that she may even decree the subversion of established rules in this particular. But, speaking subject to her correction, it may be said that good taste requires that in the in-door morning dress there should be but little positive color; that the tone be quiet, the whole style simple, graceful, and dependent for effect upon a finished and exquisite neatness in detail.

Here, as elsewhere, there must be, of course, the difference exacted by station in society. The busy little housewife, whose income is small, and who has every hour usefully employed, would appear ridiculous receiving her friends in the superb silk that may be worn with perfect propriety by her sister in the fashionable circles, with unlimited command of money, and no master but the dictates of custom to obey.

The most suitable materials, however, are those inexpensive goods which range between the chintz and silks. Linen collar and cuffs may be worn if the whole dress is of studied simplicity, but with finer material and more stylish make, lace is a more becoming finish. Elaborate trimming is out of place, and so, also, is very conspicuous jewelry.

Piqué, marseilles, cambric, lawn, and muslin, are all appropriate materials for summer wear, and in winter alpaca, poplin, delaine, merino, or cashmere, are appropriate. Trimmed neatly, with handsome collar, cuffs, and subdued jewelry, a lady will be well dressed for morning calls in any of these materials.

A lady should always avoid wearing what have been elaborate afternoon or evening dresses, partly worn, in the reception of morning calls. Shabby finery is always detestable, and never more so than in the morning. The simplest dress, fresh and appropriate, will appear much more lady-like than half-worn dresses of rich material.

Slippers are admissible, of kid, trimmed, and form a very coquettish addition if trimmed to match the dress. A simple head-dress may be worn, but no flowers, nor anything glaring or elaborate.

Many ladies adopt the dressy wrapper as a dress for the reception of morning calls, wearing it often open over an elaborately tucked or embroidered petticoat, with embroidered slippers and breakfast cap. If such a dress is worn, it must be very handsome, or it will appear out of place. Strictly speaking, as we have said before, this dress is inappopriate excepting for the dressing-room, or for an invalid receiving callers in her own room. It may then be worn with perfect propriety.

Breakfast shawls are not appropriate. They may be thrown round a breakfast dress, and serve sometimes for a finish, but as a rule they are in bad taste, and too often used to cover deficiencies, to appear well in a drawing-room, unless ill health requires their use. Even then a warmer dress will be much more becoming.

If a piece of fancy work is carried in the hand, be careful that its bright colors do not utterly ruin the effect of your dress. We have seen an exquisite dress entirely marred in effect by contrast with a vivid scarlet pin-cushion in the hands of the wearer.

OUT-DOOR DRESSES—DRIVING.

WE have already given the promenade dress under our list of costumes to be worn in the morning, and now come to another scarcely less important consideration, the morning or afternoon drive.

The dress must be governed by the strictest rules of adaptiveness, and we can give only general broad directions.

For driving in a handsome private carriage through the streets of a large city, or in the fashionable Park, the most elaborate out-door costume is expected. Richest silk, velvet, and lace are all appropriate, and elaborate style and trimming are allowable. In summer, light, thin goods, shawls of white or black lace, dainty lace bonnets, gloves of light-colored kid, light, dressy boots, collars and cuffs of fine lace, and jewelry that is rich and tasteful, are all strictly appropriate for the full-dress drive, while in cooler weather the white velvet sacque, black velvet cloak, or rich wrap of any material may be worn.

A carriage blanket of fur, or somber color, will be found more generally becoming in setting off the handsome costume suitable for a full-dress drive, than the gaudy Afghans now in vogue, which too often destroy, by inharmonious contrast, the effect of the most tasteful costumes.

Furs are a handsome winter addition to a handsome winter driving-dress, and white ones may be worn with perfect propriety if the remainder of the dress is elegant and costly. In summer a dressy little parasol for the open barouche is a pretty addition to the dress.

In the country, however, the driving-dress should be of entirely different style, as the roads are always either dusty or muddy, and the style of carriage usually different from that used in the city.

The most appropriate dress for a country drive in the summer time is linen, or some other wash goods, from which the stains of mud or dust may be afterwards removed; a straw hat, simply trimmed, and thread gloves; over the dress a large cape-or duster of linen should be worn, and even in the winter this addition will be found a most valuable protection against the mud or dust of the road. In winter a simple dress of woolen material, and dark or squirrel-skin furs, with a felt hat, forms a genteel driving-dress. If the lady drives herself, the most suitable gloves are of wash leather or chamois-skin, beaver-cloth or broadcloth. Kid or thread are too delicate to look well after contact with the reins.

Many prefer the short walking-dress for driving, and it is certainly more convenient if the carriage is small or crowded, and less liable to come in contact with the wheels. A very pretty suit is of Scotch gingham, sacque and dress alike, trimmed with broad, white marseilles braid, and marseilles buttons; a straw hat with ruche of ribbon round the crown, and thread gloves. Linen, made into a short walking-suit, is also a becoming driving-dress for the country; nankeen, marseilles, piqué, indeed any of the summer materials of rather heavy thread are all perfectly appropriate, for either young or elderly persons. Nothing of very delicate color or fabric is suitable for the country drive.

OUT-DOOR DRESSES—RIDING.

THERE is no occasion upon which a handsome, well-formed woman may appear to greater advantage than when dressed in a becoming and appropriate riding-dress. Not only the colors and materials, but the make, finish, and trimming, all allow and call for the exercise of good taste, perfect fitness, and exquisite adaptiveness. Whether for the ride in the fashionable park, where she may be the object of severe criticism or admiration, or for the quiet country road, surrounded only by Nature's beauties, a lady on horseback depends very materially upon her dress for effect. The most graceful and finished rider will appear awkward and to disadvantage if her habit fits clumsily, or makes conspicuous wrinkles, and no jewelry in her whip-handle will cover up a pair of dirty or torn gloves, or even compensate for a want of harmony in color.

The first requisite for a fair equestrienne is that the habit fit the figure perfectly, yet easily. A dress that sets loosely will never display its wrinkles so conspicuously as upon horseback, and one that is too tight is equally bad. The sleeves must be long enough to allow of some play of the arm and wrist, yet not interfere with the motions of the hand. The skirt, while full, graceful, and flowing, must avoid the extreme length, which soon becomes disfigured by the mud of the road, and is positively dangerous if of material light enough to be caught by the wind. The boots must be of stout material enough to resist the friction of the stirrup, and the gloves gauntleted and fitting the hand smoothly.

The most serviceable material for a habit is waterproof

cloth, the most dressy, fine broadcloth. In summer linen and nankeen may be worn, but should be very heavy, and the hem of the skirt shotted to keep it down.

The most becoming and appropriate riding-dress is made to fit the waist closely, and button to the throat, with sleeves (coat pattern) coming to the wrist. Linen collar and cuffs are *en règle*. If the waist is cut to open over a shirt front, the latter must be of plain fine linen, never of lace or embroidery. It is better to have the body separate from the skirt, in a basque or jacket, and to have an underskirt of the same material, the usual length for walking, that in case of any mishap to the long skirt, it may be easily removed. Many ladies have the dress made entire of walking length, and then wear over it the long riding-skirt, belted neatly at the waist.

Bright colors are not in good taste on horseback, deep blue or green, and in summer a buff, in linen or nankeen, being the most conspicuous colors allowable. The gloves must be of buckskin, or beaver cloth, and of buff, white, or neutral tint. A little liveliness in the necktie is sometimes permitted, but a narrow black ribbon is in better taste.

In the hat wear a compact shape, and avoid anything that will stream on the wind in trimming. The veil must be carefully secured, and the hair arranged as snugly as possible. However pretty and graceful floating ribbons and fluttering curls upon horseback may be in theory, in reality they will be found annoying to the rider and her escort, soon blowzy and unbecoming, and always in bad taste.

Jewelry is entirely out of place, excepting what is absolutely necessary to fasten the different parts of the dress, and what is worn must be of the plainest kind. If a feather is worn in the hat, it must be carefully secured, and held away from danger of falling over the eyes.

The whip should be carefully secured to the waist by an elastic band. Taste and richness may govern the selection of this little article, which is often made a token of friendship, and affords scope for the exercise of some coquetry in wearing. Glittering stones are not in good taste, but the handle may be finished with gold, enameled, decorated with coral, or, in short, allowing any freak of fancy in its manufacture.

The trimming for a riding-habit must invariably be flat. Ruffling, puffing, or flouncing, are all out of place. The handsomest finish is a narrow braid of black, or a perfect match for the material, sewn on in an elaborate pattern. Large buttons form an appropriate finish, and young ladies may allow their fancy some play in the selection. Fancy hairnets, gaudy hat trimmings, flashing jewelry, are never more vulgar than when exhibited in a riding-dress, while simple elegance has here one of its most appropriate opportunities for display.

As a rule, the heavy materials are the best in a habit. Alpaca is sometimes worn, but is unsuitable, being liable to tear easily, to be caught by the wind, and looking flimsy and cheap. If the weather requires a body of lighter material than is appropriate for the skirt, it must be a perfect match in color and density of material, or it will look very badly.

In winter a habit is very appropriate and handsome made of broadcloth, fitting the figure perfectly, with a basque waist, trimmed at the throat, wrists, and round the skirt, with fur; a cap of velvet the same color as the dress, or a happy contrast, trimmed with a fur band and ear-covers ; gauntlet gloves of dark cloth, embroidered, and boots of stout leather with a fur band.

In summer a dress of heavy linen, braided with fine braid, white, or the color of the dress; a straw hat, trimmed with a close plume or knots of ribbon (avoiding any dangling or floating trimming); gloves of white or buff wash-leather, and boots of kid, is handsome and appropriate.

A loose sacque or jacket is very awkward on horseback. It makes a graceful figure appear clumsy, and will conceal no defects if the figure is bad. We should recommend those who are not so fortunate as to possess a symmetrical figure, to avoid too public a display on horseback; as there is no dress in which there is so little opportunity of artistically concealing, or of veiling from prominent notice, any natural defects. Still, a lady of a most graceful figure, not completely at ease in the saddle, will often compare quite unfavorably with one less naturally gifted, but possessing the great advantage of thorough proficiency in the art of riding.

OUT-DOOR DRESSES—CHURCH.

It is too much the custom in the cities of the United States to make the house of public worship the scene for the display of finery, and to think more of the bonnets worn by ourselves or our neighbors than of the purposes for which the congregation is assembled together. To go to church "to see and be seen," it is needless to say, is the aim of too many of the fair sex, and it would be useless as well as absurd to enter upon a sermon against such vanity within the compass of our little book.

We by no means would advocate appearing in the sacred edifice in a careless, slovenly dress. It would be a gross disrespect of the place and the occasion, but we insist that the lady perfect mistress of the art of dressing well, will not select Sunday for the display of finery. A simple, modest elegance will mark her church-going costume, perfect in neatness, taste, and in finish, yet with nothing conspicuous to attract attention or provoke comment, even if admiring.

Rustling silks are especially annoying in church, as the least movement of the wearer causes them to make a noise sufficient to make inaudible for the moment the voice of the preacher. Strong perfumes are another mark of low breeding, as many of them are intensely disagreeable to some persons, one of whom may be obliged to bear the annoyance of its close proximity during the entire service.

Indeed any peculiarity that by attracting attention disturbs the devotion, or causes annoyance to others, is in the worst possible taste in church, bad enough, we admit, in any public place, but worst of all there.

Materials that make no rustling, soft woolen fabrics in winter, and noiseless fabrics in summer, will be found the most agreeable to wear in church, and can be made handsome and appropriate. If silk is worn, the heavier it is the better it will serve the purpose.

OUT-DOOR DRESSES—SKATING.

WARM tints, rich materials, and room for free play of the limbs, are all to be observed in the choice of this most coquettish of all dresses. The skirts must clear the ankle, and the sacque or basque must leave the arms perfectly free.

Velvet trimmed with fur, turban hat of the same, high kid boots with fur tops, and gloves fur-bound at the wrists, will make the richest skating costume; but more inexpensive material, tastefully made and trimmed, can be made very effective. Cashmere, broadcloth, merino, and poplin, are all suitable materials for this dress, and velvet, ribbon, gimp, in fact any trimming fashion dictates, may be worn, although nothing is so becoming, comfortable and appropriate as fur.

The boots must be sufficiently loose to allow the skate to be fastened securely without in any way cramping the foot. Not only is all grace of motion and comfort destroyed by tight boots, but the danger of frozen feet is much increased by this interference with the circulation of the blood.

The muff should be attached to a ribbon or cord and suspended from the neck, and should be quite small, just large enough to hold the hands comfortably.

Any display of jewelry is vulgar, only that necessary to finish the dress being in good taste. Jeweled clasps for the hat, feather, and other displays of the kind, are all in bad taste.

Scotch plaid for some portions of the dress, without being too prominent, has a very pretty effect.

Crimson, and the deeper shades of blue, purple, rich browns, and black, when somewhat relieved by contrasting colors, are all in better taste for the skating-dress than light blues, or greens, or any of the cold neutral tints. If green is worn, it should be of a dark shade, and relieved by rich, dark furs. Velvet of the richest quality, with mink trimming, is handsome in dark green, but trying to most complexions.

Floating ribbons, veils—unless masks in shape—fringe, or, in fact, any trimming that is apt to catch, will be found troublesome upon the ice, although they add to the grateful appearance of a finished skater.

White furs, though a beautiful finish to a rich velvet dress, are suitable for no other, and should be worn only by a skater of experience, as the novice will find them much injured by falling, and a soiled fur will ruin the handsomest dress.

Broadcloth, or any woolen material, is handsomest trimmed with dark fur, or broad folds of velvet the same color as the dress. Silk will bear white fur, but is not a material adapted for the dress, unless very heavy and corded, and of a rich, warm color. Irish poplin, of claret color, garnet, dark blue, or brown, trims well with white or dark fur, but the lighter silks are not effective or appropriate.

Fur may be worn at the throat, wrists, ankles, on the edge of the jacket, and even the edge of the skirt, on the cap or hat, and in a muff. Ear caps of fur are comfortable, and becoming.

OUT-DOOR DRESSES—PICNIC.

The picnic dress is by no means so simple a costume to arrange as may at first appear. Picnic is a word that invites the company to an entire day spent in the open air, fine weather being understood, but not invariably attained. In selecting the dress it is fair to conclude that summer fabric is most suitable, yet a north-east rain or a heavy thunder-storm may send the wearer of pretty muslin or lawn shivering home to occupy a sick bed. Even supposing the day fair throughout, the light fabric, so becoming and pretty in the morning, may be caught by bush or brier, stained by fruit or grass, and present a most woe-begone appearance by noon.

The main objects are comfort, suitability, and beauty, and to combine the three is a practice in the art of dressing well by no means to be despised. Wash material is the best, thin enough for comfort on a warm day, inexpensive enough for full freedom, stout enough to resist thorns and branches, and yet admitting of taste in the color and fashion. The great variety of such fabrics will allow of a display of taste in the selection, even if the cheapest of chintz is worn.

French cambric is one of the prettiest materials that can be selected for a picnic dress. It is light and cool, yet stout enough to bear some pulling and straining; it washes well, and can be made in pretty fashion.

A broad hat, completely shading the face, thick-soled boots, and a waterproof cloak, should always form portions of a picnic dress. Parasols and umbrellas are thereby rendered superfluous, and they are always awkward additions. Lawn, muslin, and the varieties of white dress goods, make beautiful picnic dresses, but are apt to suffer severely if there is much climbing or active out-door exercise.

Trailing skirts are out of place, but pretty gay ribbons may be worn, and are effective. Light, gay colors, happily blended or contrasted, are perfectly appropriate. Many ladies display a coquettish taste in a dainty little white apron worn while dinner is preparing and eaten, and then packed away in the lunch-basket. Gloves are best of white thread, that may be afterwards washed, but gloves at a picnic are not *de rigeur*, and may be left at home if the hand does not tan easily.

There are numerous cosmetics for removing the tan, freckles, etc., that are apt to follow a day spent on a picnic, but the best preventives are gloves, a broad hat, and a material for the dress thick enough to protect perfectly the neck and arms.

OUT-DOOR DRESSES---TRAVELING.

A LADY's dress is never more exposed to criticism than when she is traveling, and there is no surer index of her taste and skill in the art of dressing well than is shown in this important costume. Vulgarity of taste will dictate a conspicuous style, utterly abhorrent to a refined eye, while quiet elegance is never more attractive than in a traveling companion.

Jewelry, artificial flowers, lace, or finery of any kind in a traveling-dress, will prove the most vulgar desire for display, and conspicuous colors are in as bad taste.

The great variety of goods now sold expressly for traveling-suits, affords full scope for the display of taste in a selection. Neutral tints are *de rigeur*, and a large linen duster is always a desirable wrap to protect the suit. In summer linen is most comfortable, and has the advantage of cleanliness, as it can be washed often and look well. In winter, waterproof cloth, a dress and loose sacque, will be found the most serviceable wear. Thread gloves in summer, and cloth in winter, are preferable to kid. If furs are worn, squirrel skin will show the dust least, and are most economical, as expensive furs are often badly injured by the dust, dampness, and crushing of traveling.

A traveling-dress should always be made quite short, and the underskirts should be of woolen in winter, and dark linen in summer; white petticoats will not look well but a very short time on a journey.

Strong, thick-soled kid boots should always be worn in traveling, even in summer.

The hat or bonnet must be trimmed compactly, without feathers or flowers, and protected by a thick barege veil.

As no lady can appear well dressed in crushed or rumpled clothing, the following directions for packing a trunk are added, that all may be fresh at the end of a journey:

To pack a trunk neatly, everything should be laid out in readiness, neatly folded and sorted, the light articles divided from the heavy ones, and a supply of towels and soft wrapping-paper at hand. Spread a thick, clean towel over the bottom of the trunk, and place upon it the hard, flat things, such as the portfolio, work-box, jewel-box, music-books, writing-desk, and boxes; take care to fit them well together, so as to be level on top, filling in crevices with such small articles as will not be injured by compressment, as stockings, towels or flannels. Wrap all polished boxes in soft paper before packing, and guard the corners well from rubbing against each other. Never use newspapers in packing, as they will certainly ruin whatever clothing rubs against them.

In packing shoes, it is best to have a shoe-bag, or two pieces of calico bound together and divided into pockets, each large enough to hold one shoe. Spread this flat over the bottom of the trunk, if there is room left by the flat hard articles.

Over this first layer spread another towel, and then put in your flannels, linen, such dresses and petticoats as will bear pressure, and any paper boxes for gloves, handkerchiefs, or perfumes. On top of these put the more dressy petticoats, and handsome dresses, unless your trunk has a tray in the lid expressly for this purpose. If the trunk has no bonnet-box, put your bandbox in near the top. In the tray put collars, muslins, handkerchiefs, and a supply of writing-paper, and envelopes, a box of sewing materials, your laces, ribbons, gloves, parasol-box, veils, and any light articles you may wish to carry.

To fold a dress for packing, spread it, right side out, upon the bed, and taking it by the hem, make the bottom exactly even all round. Next, double the skirt in half, lengthwise, and then in four, reversing the fourth fold. After this, turn up), crossways, about one-third of the folded lower part of the skirt, then give the remainder of the skirt a fold backward, terminating at the waist. Then turn the body backward, front uppermost, and the back resting on the folded skirt. Spread out the sleeves, give each a fold forward at the shoulder, and backward at the elbow, and then lay them evenly across the body. Place the dress so folded upon a large clean towel, and fold this smoothly over it before placing it in the trunk.

Under-clothing of all kinds will look much better at the end of a journey if folded instead of rolled, and will pack quite as easily.

Shawls, cloaks, sacques, and veils, should be folded in their original folds before packing; gloves should be drawn out smooth and put in a glove-box. Collars and cuffs must lie in the tray, or, better still, in a paper box.

A bonnet will look better after a journey if the flowers or feathers are taken out and carried separately in a paper box, and the strings are smoothly rolled, not folded, upon pasteboard.

Leave always room in your trunk for a bag to receive soiled linen, if your journey is to be a long one.

The traveling-dress should be always of material strong enough to bear some severe jerking and straining, and dark enough to conceal dust or spots, unless it is of material that will wash. It should fit easily, and a sacque of the same material is always best. Pockets in the sacque as well as the dress are convenient, and a strong pocket in the under-skirt is advisable. A collar and cuffs of plain linen, fastened by a simple brooch and buttons, kid boots, and strong gloves, are in the best taste. A hat is generally more convenient than a bonnet, and should be of straw in summer, and felt in winter, simply trimmed. Any fancy material, lace or velvet, is in excessively bad taste in a traveling-hat.

In addition, a well-dressed lady will be provided with a large linen cape or duster, a heavy blanket shawl, a thick barege veil, a waterproof cloak, and carry in her satchel an extra pair of boots and gloves, clean collar and cuffs.

Shepherd's plaid, trimmed with fluted ruffles of the same, or with flat black braid, is a pretty and cheap material for traveling suits, and if of good material, has the advantage of washing well.

If the journey is to be a long one, and there is a great deal of hand-luggage required, the duster will be found much more convenient made into a long sacque, wide enough in the skirt to perfectly cover and protect the entire dress, and furnished with large, deep pockets. The veil is a more perfect protection if the elastic string is run through the middle, put over the hat and under the chin, allowing the veil to fall front and back.

It is in better taste to wear the hair in smooth, compact style, than in curls or any flowing fashion, and it will be more likely to escape injury by railroad cinders and the dust of travel.

When a journey is to be very long, especially in the winter, colored stockings, colored linen corsets, and colored skirts, will be found much more serviceable than white ones, especially if there is no stop to be made for washing. Soiled linen in a trunk is a most disagreeable addition, and it is not always convenient to carry a satchel for this purpose in the hand. For a sea-voyage it is best to carry an extra trunk especially for under-clothing, keeping the top and tray for soiled clothes.

OUT-DOOR DRESSES FOR STORMY WEATHER.

EVERY lady expert in the art of dressing well will be provided with a full suit of seasonable clothing for stormy weather, as there is nothing looks worse than expensive or dressy clothing worn under a cloudy sky or in a heavy storm. The material for a storm suit should be rather heavy, even in summer time, and a waterproof cloak is a valuable addition. The aqua scutum cloth varies so much in thickness that it can be worn at all seasons with comfort, and while it can be obtained quite light enough for a storm wrap in summer, it is also manufactured heavy enough for the entire dress in winter.

The storm-dress must be short, not very full, and made with a close-fitting sacque to leave the arms free. The cloak must have a large hood to entirely cover the hat or bonnet. Heavy-soled boots of waterproof leather, coming high on the leg, and in a snow-storm india rubber boots are indispensable. The petticoat is best made of aqua scutum cloth, short, and bound with the same.

In summer a stout linen, trimmed with flat, white braid, is the most serviceable storm-suit, as it can be washed if wet or muddied, and the petticoat is best made of the same material.

If an umbrella is carried, the gloves should be dark and of strong material; kid is ruined by an umbrella.

It is a mistaken idea to suppose that "any old thing will do to wear in rainy weather." The well-dressed lady will present as neat and appropriate an appearance in a storm as on

the clearest day. She will never appear on the street in a
soiled, half-worn dress of by-gone beauty, dragging a trail,
perhaps, in the mud; a bonnet of faded splendor, and old kid-
gloves, with the fingers peeping out at various open points.
You never see her dragging muddy white petticoats through
the rain-puddles, and showing a soaked gaiter-boot at every
step. Every article she wears will be fit for the occasion,
and she will come home as dry and comfortable under her
waterproof cloak and with her waterproof boots as if she had
taken her walk in the sunshine.

If, however, old dresses are reserved for storm-suits, they
should be made short, divested of all superfluous trimming,
and be of serviceable material. Flimsy goods will not bear
stormy weather, and silk, if old, can be put to many better
uses, while one or two hard rains would utterly ruin it.

The dress worn in a storm should be taken off as soon as
possible, spread out to dry, and well aired before it is put
away. It will improve the appearance of most dresses to
be pressed before wearing again, and all should be thoroughly
brushed.

GENTLEMEN'S DRESS.

It is a proverb in France that "It is not the cowl which
makes the monk," so "it is not the dress which makes the
gentleman;" yet, as the monk is known by his cowl, so may
the innate refinement that distinguishes the gentleman from
the clown be known by his costume. It is not always the
broad distinction between the sloven and the coxcomb that
the dress decides, but those finer shades of difference that
proven a habitual care in dress that will safely avoid the one
without becoming the other.

As men dress in the present day, there is but little that can
be said of color in relation to their ordinary habiliments.
Had it been our fortune to write in the days of past glories,
when the well-dressed gentleman kept in his wardrobe his
several suits of brown velvet and silver, of blue satin and
gold, of green velvet slashed with white satin and embroidered in scarlet; coats of cherry-colored calimanco, and peach-
blossom hose; endless varieties of embroidered waistcoats;
silk stockings of every hue, and breeches of numerous shades,
it might have taxed our ingenuity to draw the line where vulgarity begins and artistic taste ends.

We must take things as they are.

It is generally said, and it must be owned, with a great
deal of apparent truth, that gentlemen of the present day
dress worse than ladies, and yet make a greater parade of

their finery. One is a necessary consequence of the other. We are all vainer of the arts in which we are only smatterers, than of those in which we are proficient. Who ever shows his hideous caricatures of the human countenance. and libelous "sketches from Nature," with half the smirking complacency of the self-taught amateur? Ladies do, as a rule, give some steady thought to matters of dress, its harmony, fitness, fashion, and with a view to the adoption of what is most suitable to their own personal appearance, pecularities of figure, complexion, and age.

Gentlemen, however, as a rule, when they do give any attention to the subject, give it in such a languid, jerky, disconnected, superficial sort of way, that, with all their tedious care, they only succeed in dressing so as to render themselves conspicuous.

Now we are certainly not of the opinion that dress is a matter to which it is advisable for young men to give a great amount of serious consideration. There may indeed be some who have nothing better to do; who dawdle away the valuable hours in the club-room, the drawing-room, or the billiard-room, and whose evenings can be put, apparently, to no better use than lounging at the opera, or in the concert-room. These may find their tailor their most absorbing and interesting companion, and dwell with emphasis upon the last cut for a vest, or the merits of rival neck-ties.

But such devotion to dress is unmanly. There are few things, not actually immoral, less to be desired than the name or character of a fop. Most young men, however, who have a reasonable conceit of themselves, pass through what has been called the "dandy stage" in youth, just as in childhood they are subject to measles, whooping-cough, and scarlet fever. Some excess in dress is then, at least, pardonable; and as consideration will be given to the question of how to dress, it is perhaps well that such consideration should be intelligent. This will soon yield a man as much knowledge on the subject as he will need. He will not have to watch what form or color of dress some acknowledged leader of fashion has lately adopted, or be entirely at the mercy of his associates or his tailor, as to the fashion of his coat, but will dress fitly and becomingly from habit, or, as Bacon said of a kindred matter, "by a kind of felicity (as a musician that maketh an excellent air in music), and not by rule."

There is but little danger that a man who has much in his head and heart worth cultivating will persist long in devoting much time, thought, or attention to dress. But the advantage of acquiring once for all the art of dressing *well*, is. that once gained, a man will continue to dress in a fit and becoming style by a sort of intuition; whilst, if it is never acquired, he will attire himself awkwardly or conspicuously, with a great deal of trouble; or, if he take no care, will fall into the disgusting extreme of a sloven by habit.

This habit of being well dressed will cover the necessities of daily toilet cares, the first of which is appropriateness. In this connection a gentleman's age is a most important consideration; a man of sixty is as unutterably absurd in the height of a prevailing fashion, as a lad of nineteen would be in the breeches and long stockings of the past century. As a general rule, a man who has passed middle age, while he tolerates frequent changes of fashion in his sons, should avoid them in his own attire. The young man, on the other hand, should exercise some judgment in following the caprices of fashion, and, while avoiding eccentricity of costume, consult taste and position in his selection of clothing. Any new fashion which imparts additional grace, ease, comfort, and convenience, is certainly to be desired. Greater freedom in any garment will be gladly hailed, while foppish extravagancies are utterly discarded and ignored.

Some regard must be paid to profession and position in society. Many a man is judged, however unjustly, merely by his appearance, and although much outcry has been made at this test, it certainly proves two points—tact and discretion. Position in society demands some regard to appearance, and this a man of the world will give easily and gracefully, never following every absurd freak of fashion in every minute detail of dress, yet avoiding such solecisms as will mark carelessness, meanness, or disregard of the prevailing modes appropriate to the time, place and season.

The great principle of dressing well, according to the style of dress now prevailing amongst gentlemen, is simplicity. Alike in the shape and make of the several garments, the materials, the colors, the *tout ensemble*, simplicity is the rule. This strict simplicity is really the sole distinction in dress to which a man of taste should aspire, but simplicity of style requires most accurate nicety in detail; one must be simply well-dressed, not carelessly ill-dressed. When Lord Castlereagh was in Vienna, and was known as the most distinguished-looking man in the gay court, it was not simply because he wore no profusion of orders or decorations, when others were glittering with them, but because his exquisite nicety of costume had attained the perfection of strict simplicity. So with Brummel, that prince of dandies. For the age in which he lived, his dress was extremely simple, yet he gave his whole time and attention to its finish of detail.

Taste, therefore, is synonymous with simplicity. Splendor,

extravagance and eccentricity must all be shunned. Colors must be most carefully selected, if any are worn, and must suit complexion, hair, eyes, and general appearance. It may seem superfluous to tell a gentleman of to-day not to wear red, yellow or blue, and probably no one but a lunatic would wear a coat or trousers of such colors, but the vagaries in gloves, vests and neckties are often startling in their glaring hues and vulgar contrasts.

Looking at some of the lately prevalent fashions, it may seem as if simplicity of dress was confined to the staid and middle-aged, and utterly disregarded by the young; but there are oscillations in the most stable customs. In youth there is often, if not always, some tendency to exaggeration; and, allowing for that, it will be found that simplicity is even now the governing principle of a gentleman's customary dress. This being so, the man who will study simplicity, who will utterly discard whatever savors of peculiarity and pretension, and will dress in a manly, becoming and unaffected way, will probably find that, unconsciously, he is dressing well. But a young man may be reminded that in dress, as in all else, he should cultivate manliness and gentlemanliness as a part of the respect he owes to himself; and neatness and propriety with reference to place and occasion, as marking his sense of the respect due to society.

It may be said that necessarily the principles of color, of harmony and contrast, and the laws which regulate the arrangements of color with reference to dress, apply to the wardrobe of a gentleman as they do to that of a lady, and it would therefore be but a useless repetition to give again the rules already laid down in this volume. The subject has been thoroughly treated in detail in previous chapters.

But we may say a few words of the nice distinction in dress upon special occasions—what is to be worn at dinner, the evening party, the opera, the social gatherings, in full dress, in the streets, and in the house? Much of this may be learned from intercourse with good society, from consultation with an accomplished female relative, or the Book of Etiquette, but a few hints taken from an English work upon this subject will apply equally well to American society.

"A well-dressed man," he says, "does not require so much an extensive as a well varied wardrobe. He wants a different costume for every season, and for every occasion; but if what he selects is simple rather than striking, he may appear in the same clothes as often as he likes, as long as they are fresh, and appropriate to the season and the object. There are four kinds of coat which he must have; a morning coat, a frock coat, a dress coat, and an overcoat. An economical man will do well with two of the first, and one of each of the others.

"In his own house, and in the morning, there is no reason why he should not wear out his old clothes. Some men, indeed, prefer the delicious ease of a dressing-gown and slippers, and morning visitors are kind enough to excuse them, especially in elderly or literary men.

"The best walking-dress is a suit of tweed, all of the same color, ordinary boots, gloves not too dark for the coat, a scarf with a pin for winter, or a small tie of one color in summer, a respectable black hat and cane. The main point of the walking-dress is the harmony of colors, but this should not be carried to the extent of M. de Maltzan, who some years ago made a bet to wear nothing but pink, at Baden Baden, for a whole year, and had boots and gloves of the same lively hue. He won his wager, but also the soubriquet of '*Le Diable enflamme.*'

"The walking-dress should vary according to the place and hour. In the country or at the seaside, a straw hat or a wide-awake may take the place of the beaver, and the nuisance of gloves be even dispensed with in the former. But in the city, where a man is supposed to make visits as well as lounge in the street, the frock-coat, faultless trousers and vest, and kid-gloves, are indispensable. Very thin boots should be avoided at all times, and whatever clothes one wears they should be well brushed."

In ordinary half-dress, or what might be designated the frock-coat costume, a little liberty is allowed; but not much, beyond some variety of dark color in the coat, can be ventured on without attracting notice. Not long ago, some would occasionally indulge in a frock-coat of deep claret or of plum color, and very well it looked if the rest of the dress was adapted to it; but care must be taken even in such innocent wanderings.

Black is, of course, always safe, and black is generally becoming to a gentleman, be he of light, dark or florid complexion ; but where color may be ventured upon, color is often preferable. With light trousers a light waistcoat always accords best ; the trousers should be of a quiet neutral tint. Patterns are dangerous and apt to vulgarize any costume. Every now and then colored waistcoats come into fashion. Should the fashion recur, it must be remembered that the colors should be carefully chosen, and with reference to form and features, hair and complexion, and patterns must be still more carefully selected. Bright-colored vests are very apt to look vulgar and out of keeping with the rest of the attire. They had better be left to fast young men and flourishing *parvenus*. The same may be said of gaudy-figured neck-scarfs, fastened with a staring pin. These are intensely vulgar, wherever and whenever seen, and a man of taste will invariably discard them.

Colored neck-scarfs are very well at proper seasons, but never gaudy ones. If worn, they should be quiet, plain, or at the most of an unobtrusive pattern and of a color that will perfectly harmonize with the coat and waistcoat, and not seriously disaccord with complexion, mustache or beard—if the latter hirsute appendage be indulged in. The effect, for instance, of a sandy beard, will never be improved by a brilliant red or yellow neck-scarf. With a colored scarf the waistcoat should not be too open, and the pin should be of moderate size, and its head either artistic in pattern, or a small gem. If a narrow necktie be preferable, the bow must not be too formal, nor the ends too long. Some years ago, ribbons were worn for neckties, and were actually worn of the brightest colors two yards long. With the narrow tie a more open waistcoat may be worn than with the scarf, but not so open as to make a marked display of shirt front.

The linen on all occasions must be scrupulously neat, devoid of all niminy-piminy insertion, embroidery or finery, and the studs plain, but such as will bear examination as fair examples of art, workmanship and good taste.

Thus dressed for the city promenade, it will be a young man's own fault if he is not presentable. His appearance will, at any rate, at first commend him, even if his conversation cancels instead of improving the first impression.

In a walking dress, where no calls are to be made, where you adhere to a frock-coat, one of very dark color, not black, will be best, and with it trousers and vest of gray or other light color, or at the proper season an entire suit of some quiet neutral tint or mixed goods. A wash waistcoat is also allowable of white, buff or some pale hue, as the very light greenish-gray worn a year or two ago.

Bright colored gloves are an utter abomination. The undress walking or country suit requires to be obviously easy, appropriate and convenient. The shooting jacket, under almost any of the hundred and one tailor's varieties, is a manly and universally becoming garment. When of one color, and the waistcoat and trousers of another and lighter hue, the effect is decidedly better than when all are cut from the same piece, or the coat and waistcoat are of one, and the trousers of a different color; but in this fashion will generally carry the day.

Large patterns are simply detestable; few men look well in

them, and most are utterly vulgarized by their use. They are distinctive of a racing, gambling set of men generally, and entirely avoided by gentlemen. The usual costume for traveling, promenade, morning meeting for archery, croquet, or other out-door pursuit, worn by a well-dressed man will be always extremely simple. The coat must be loose, the trousers easy; the hat of soft felt, or a comfortable straw or low cloth hat is best, with sufficient brim to shade the eyes. Tightly fitting suits and hard, flat-brimmed hats should be left to jockeys, who may also appropriate the gaudy neckties, and brilliant waistcoats.

Evening dress, being confined to black and white, may, as far as color is concerned, be left unnoticed. Only we may express a wish that some gentleman of sufficiently pre-eminent position would have good taste and decision enough to break through the absurd restriction. Every gentleman feels the absurdity of disguising himself like an undertaker or a waiter, every time he goes to a dress party, and yet no one has the courage to exchange the gloomy attire for one more suited to himself and the festive occasion. Drawing-rooms must have looked very different in our grandfathers' days.

As it is, there is nothing to be done but to take care that the costume is marked by an air of ease, refinement, appropriateness, and quiet good taste.

For all evening-dress black cloth trousers, waistcoat and coat are *de regueur;* the necktie for a ball, opera, and soirée must be white, of silk or fine linen cambric, without embroidery; for smaller evening parties the black silk-tie is allowable, but must be small and perfectly simple. The shirt front must be plain, in small or broad plaits, according to taste. Gloves must be white. Some indeed wear delicately tinted gloves, but white is the rule.

There are additions, however, that will go far to spoil the effect of even the most exquisitely arranged dress. The wearing a number of rings is always a mark of effeminacy, and too often the rings are ill-matched. Only one ring at a time should ever be worn. A signet or a mourning ring is allowable to any one, but if the former, it should be of artistic value, unless it is valuable as a souvenir. Almost the only gem ring that is becoming to a manly hand, is a moderate-sized diamond, and that is less suitable than either of those already mentioned. The bunch of meaningless trinkets it is so usual to see dangling at the waistcoat—charms that have no charm in them for any eyes but those of the wearer—would be best dispensed with altogether. If some are worn, remember that the fewer there are the better will be the effect, and the only way to justify the taste in wearing them at all, is to wear such as are of artistic value, if such can be found.

At the risk of repetition we give a few hints on jewelry from the English authority before quoted. He says:

" Jewels are an ornament to women, but a blemish to men. They bespeak either effeminacy, or a love of display. The hand of a man is honored in working, for labor is his mission; and the hand that wears its riches on its fingers has rarely worked honestly to win them. The best jewel a man can wear is his honor. Let that be bright and shining, well set in prudence, and all others must darken before it. But as we are savages, and must have some silly trickery to hang about us, a little, but very little, concession may be made to our taste in this respect. I am quite serious when I disadvise you from the use of nose-rings, gold anklets, and hat-bands studded with jewels ; for when I see a young man of this nineteenth century dangling from his watch-chain a dozen silly charms (often the only ones he possesses), which have no other use than to give a fair coquette a legitimate subject on which to open a silly flirtation, and which are revived from the lowest superstitions of dark ages, and sometimes darker races, 1 am justified in believing that some South African chieftain, sufficiently rich to cut a dash, might introduce with success the most peculiar fashions of his own country. However this may be, there are already sufficient extravagances prevalent among our young men to attack.

" The man of good taste will wear as little jewelry as possible. One handsome signet ring on the little finger of the left hand, a scarf-pin which is neither large nor showy, nor too intricate in its design, and a light, rather thin watch-guard, with a cross-bar, are all that he ought to wear. But, if he aspires to more than this, he should observe the following rules:

" First: Let everything be real and good. False jewelry is not only a practical lie, but an absolute vulgarity, since its use arises from an attempt to appear richer or grander than its wearer is.

" Secondly: Let it be simple. Elaborate studs, waistcoat buttons, and wrist links, are all abominable. The last, particularly, should be as plain as possible, consisting of plain gold ovals, with, at most, the initials engraved upon them. Diamonds and brilliants are quite unsuitable to men, whose jewelry should never be conspicuous. If you happen to possess a single diamond of great value, you may wear it on great occasions as a ring, but no more than one ring should ever be worn by a gentleman.

" Thirdly: Let it be distinguished rather by its curiosity

than its brilliance. An antique or bit of old jewelry possesses more interest, particularly if you are able to tell its history, than the most splendid modern production of the goldsmith's shop.

"Fourthly: Let it harmonize with the colors of your dress.

"Fifthly: Let it have some use. Men should never, like women, wear jewels for mere ornament, whatever may be the fashion of Hungarian nobles and deposed Indian rajahs with jackets covered with rubies.

"The precious stones are reserved for ladies, and even the scarf-pins are more suitable without them.

"The dress that is both appropriate and simple can never offend, nor render its wearer conspicuous, though it may distinguish him for his good taste. But it will not be pleasing unless clean and fresh. We cannot quarrel with a poor gentleman's threadbare coat, if his linen be pure, and we see that he has never attempted to dress beyond his means, or unsuitably to his station. But the sight of decayed gentility and dilapidated fashion may call forth our pity, and, at the same time, prompt a moral.

"'You have evidently sunken,' we say to ourselves. 'But whose fault is it? Am I not led to suppose that the extravagance which you evidently once reveled in has brought you to what I now see you?'

"While freshness is essential to being well dressed, it will be a consolation to those who cannot afford a heavy tailor's bill, to reflect that a visible newness in one's clothes is as bad as patches and darns, and to remember that there have been celebrated dressers who would never put on a new coat till it had been worn two or three times by their valets. On the other hand, there is no excuse for untidiness, holes in the boots, a broken hat, torn gloves, and so on. Indeed, it is better to wear no gloves at all than a pair full of holes. There is nothing to be ashamed of in a pair of bare hands, if they are clean, and the poor can still afford to have their shirts and shoes mended, and their hats ironed. It is certainly better to show signs of neatness than the reverse, and you need sooner be ashamed of a hole than of a darn.

"If you are economical with your tailor, you can be extravagant with your laundress. The beau of forty years back put on three shirts a day, but, except in hot weather, one is sufficient. Of course, if you change your dress in the evening, you must change your linen too. Quantity is better than quality in linen. Nevertheless, it should be fine and well spun. The loose cuff, which we borrowed from the French some few years ago, is a great improvement on the old tight wristband, and, indeed, it must be borne in mind that anything which binds any part of the body tightly, impedes the circulation, and is, therefore, unhealthy as well as ungraceful.

"The necessity for a large stock of linen depends on a rule far better than Brummel's of three shirts a day, viz:

"Change your linen whenever it is at all dirty.

"This is the best guide with regard to collars, socks, pocket-handkerchiefs, and under-garments. No rule can be laid down for the number we should wear per week, for everything depends upon circumstances. Thus, in the coun-try, all linen remains longer clean than in town; in dirty, wet, or dusty weather, our socks get soon dirty, and must be often changed; or, if we have a cold, to say nothing of the possible, but not probable, case of tear-shedding, on the departure of friends, we shall want more than one pocket-handkerchief per diem. In fact, the last article of modern civilization is put to so many uses, is so much displayed, and liable to be called into action on so many various engagements, that we should always have a clean one in our pockets. Who knows when it may not serve us in good stead? Who can tell how often the corner of the delicate cambric will have to represent a tear, which, like difficult passages in novels, is 'left to the imagination?' Can a man of any feeling call on a disconsolate widow, for instance, and listen to her woes, without at least pulling out that expressive appendage? Can any one believe in our sympathy if the article in question is a dirty one? There are some people who, like the clouds, only exist to weep, and King Solomon, though not one of them, has given them great encouragement in speaking of the house of mourning. We are bound to weep with them, and we are bound to weep elegantly.

"Elegance, however, in the handkerchief, must consist entirely in its own delicacy of texture and snowy whiteness. For a gentleman to carry an embroidered or laced pocket-handkerchief is an absurd affectation, and a colored-bordered one is vulgar in the extreme. A broad hem-stitched border is indeed allowable, and the initials or monogram may be embroidered in white in one corner, but no further ornament is in good taste. The size is also to be considered; a very small one has an effeminate appearance, while one of extra large size makes a man look as if he was carrying a sheet or a table-cloth. The medium gentleman's handkerchief is the most elegant size.

"I must not close this chapter without assuring myself that my reader knows more on its subject now than he did before. I take it for granted that he knows what it is to be in a dress-suit and in an undress costume. To be in an undress, is to be dressed for work and ordinary occupations; to wear a coat which you do not fear to spoil, and a necktie which your ink-stand will not object to, but your acquaintances might. To be dressed, on the other hand, since by dress we show our re-spect for society at large, or the persons with whom we are to mingle, is to be clothed in the garments which said society pronounces to be suitable to particular occasions; so that evening-dress in the morning, morning-dress in the evening, and a scarlet coat for walking, may all be called undress, if not positively bad dress. But there are shades of being 'dressed,' and a man is called 'little dressed,' 'well dressed,' and 'much dressed,' not according to the quantity, but the quality of his coverings.

"To be 'little dressed,' is to wear old things, of a make that is no longer the fashion, having no pretension of ele-gance, artistic beauty, or ornament. It is also to wear loung-ing clothes on occasions which demand some amount of pre-cision. To be 'much dressed' is to be in the extreme of the fashion, with brand new clothing, jewelry, and ornaments, with a touch of extravagance and gayety in your colors. Thus to wear patent leather boots and yellow gloves in a quiet morning stroll is to be much dressed, and certainly does not differ immensely from being badly dressed. To be 'well dressed' is the happy medium between these two, which is not given to every one to hold, inasmuch as good taste is a rare gift, and is a *sine qua non* thereof. Thus, while you avoid ornament and all fastness, you must cultivate fashion, that is, *good style*, in the make of your clothes. A man must not be made by his tailor, but should make him, educate him, give him his own good taste. To be well dressed is to be dressed precisely as the occasion, place, weather, your height, figure, position, age, complexion, and, remember it, your *means* require. It is to be clothed without peculiarity, pre-tension, or eccentricity; without violent colors, elaborate or-naments, or senseless fashions, introduced often by tailors, for their own profit. Good dressing is to wear as little jew-elry as possible, to be scrupulously neat, clean, and fresh. and to carry your clothes as if you did not give them a thought.

"Then, too, there is a scale of honor among clothes, which must not be forgotten. Thus, a new coat is more honorable than an old one, a shooting-coat than a dressing-gown, a frock-coat than a shooting-coat, a tail-coat than a frock-coat. There is no honor at all in a blue swallow-tailed coat, except on an old gentleman who will wear the accompaniment of brass buttons and a buff waistcoat.

"There is more honor in an old uniform than in a new one.

in one with a bullet hole in it, than in one unstained or un-spotted.

"There is more honor in a fustian jacket and smock-frock than in a dress-coat, because they are types of labor, which is far more honorable than lounging.

"Again, light clothes are generally placed above dark ones, because they cannot be so long worn, and are, therefore, proofs of expenditure, *alias* money, which in this world is a commodity more honored than every other; but, on the other hand, tasteful dress is always more honorable than that which is only costly. Light gloves are more esteemed than dark ones, and the prince of glove colors is, undeniably, lavender.

"'I should say Jones was a fast man,' said a friend to me one day, 'for he wears a white hat.' If this idea of my com-panion's be right, fastness in dress may be said to consist mainly in peculiarity. There is certainly only one step from the sublimity of fastness to the ridiculousness of snobbery, and it is not always easy to say where the one ends, and the other begins.

"A dandy, on the other hand, is the clothes on a man not a man in clothes, a living lay-figure, who displays much dress, and is quite satisfied if you praise that without taking heed of him. A sloven is in the opposite extreme; never dressed enough, and always very carelessly; but he is as bad as the other.

"The off-hand style of dress suits only an off-hand char-acter. It was, at one time, the fashion to affect a certain neg-ligence, which was called poetic, and supposed to be the re-sult of genius. An ill-tied, if not positively untied cravat was a sure sign of an unbridled imagination; and a waistcoat was held together by one button only, as if the swelling soul in the wearer's bosom had burst all the rest. If, in addition to this, the hair was unbrushed and curly, you were certain of passing for a 'man of soul.' I should not recommend any young man to adopt this style, even if he can mouth a great deal, and has a bountiful stock of quotations from the poets. It is of no use to show me the clouds. unless I can positively see you in them, and no amount of negligence in your dress or person will convince me you are a genius, unless you pro-duce an octavo volume of poems published by yourself. I con-fess I am glad that the *néglige* style, so common in novels of a few years ago, has been succeeded by neatness. What we want is real ease in the clothes, and, for my part, I should rejoice to see the Knickerbocker style generally adopted.

"Besides the ordinary occasions already mentioned, there are other special occasions requiring a change of dress. Most of our sports, together with marriage (which some people include in sports) come under this head.

"In sporting dress, the less change we make the better, where, if we are dressed *too* accurately, we are liable to be subjected to a comparison between our skill and our clothes; for shooting and fishing it is not good taste to be very well dressed. An old coat with large pockets, gaiters or large boots, with thick soles, a wide-awake hat, and at the end of the day a well-filled bag or basket, make a respectable sportsman.

"For cricket and base-ball you want a flannel suit, quite plain, a flannel cap, and shoes with spikes in them, unless you belong to a club and wear a uniform.

"For riding, the trousers must be firmly strapped under the boot, and a cap is more comfortable than a hat.

"Skating requires a loose dress, for perfect grace and ease of motion; a fur cap is allowable and fur gloves, and an overcoat should always be in readiness to put on as soon as the violent exercise is over.

"Sailing or rowing, like base-ball, is apt to include a club uniform. If not, a flannel shirt, with a collar of the same, black neck-tie and heavy trousers, will be at once comfortable and appropriate.

"Traveling suits are best protected by a long, loose, linen overcoat and duster, with a high stand-up collar that may be buttoned close to protect the white collar and neck-tie under it.

"The dress for a bridegroom differs but little from a full-dress morning costume. The days are gone by when gentlemen were married in white satin breeches and waistcoat. ' In these days men show less joy in their attire at the fond consummation of their hopes, and more in their faces. A very dark blue frock-coat, or a black one, although many consider the latter color worn at a wedding ominous, trousers of the same, a white waistcoat, and, in some cases, light trousers suffice for the 'happy man.' The neck-tie should be of white linen cambric, perfectly plain. Patent leather boots are not amiss, but well polished ones are also appropriate; the day of pumps is happily over. White kid gloves are a rule. Gloves and linen of spotless purity are typical—for in these days types are as important as under Hebrew law-givers—of the similar purity of the heart and mind which are supposed to exist in the wearer. After all, a bridegroom cannot be too well dressed, for the more gay he is the greater the compliment to the bride, so for once, he may don diamond studs, his diamond ring, handsome watch chain, and even put a flower in his button-hole, to show the exultations of his heart.

Colors he may not wear in his waistcoat or neck-tie, but if he is afraid of a black coat, by all means let him wear a dark-colored one."

The mourning-dress usually worn by a gentleman is a full suit of black broadcloth, a crape band round the hat, of depth governed by the closeness of the black worn, and jet studs and cuff buttons. A widower wears a band the width of his hat, and this is the deepest mourning worn. The fashion, prevalent we know, of wearing only the crape hat-band for mourning, and the rest of the dress of the usual light or dark colors, has the advantages only of convenience and economy, but is making a farce of mourning; it would be quite as appropriate for a lady to wear a suit of colored clothes, with a heavy crape veil thrown over her bonnet. If mourning is worn at all, the entire dress should be of black. A straw hat is allowable in summer, with the crape band, and in lighter mourning gloves of dark gray or of lavender are suitable; studs of pearl set in jet, or jet bound with gold, are also worn in lighter mourning-dress, while the hat-band is cut narrower as the rest of the dress is lightened.

If a gentleman in summer indulges in the luxury of full suits of white linen, it is imperative that they be of spotless whiteness. Such a dress is a *luxury* at best, and to wear it more than once is impossible, as it will show signs at once of even a few hours' wear.

There are two articles of a gentleman's dress to which too much attention cannot be given—a neat hat, and a pair of *clean*, well-fitting boots. The remark has been made in connection with ladies' dress, that there is absolute economy in a well-fitting shoe or gaiter; the same is still more applicable to gentlemen, as they are likely to have more out-door exercise. An ill-fitting boot, however bright and spotless it may be, will mar the effect of the most careful toilet, and will wear out much faster both themselves and the stockings inside them.

The high hat is the only covering suitable to *all* occasions. Fashions change and differ in all other styles, and these may only be used in connection with a walking or business suit; they cannot be worn by any one who cares at all for appearances, when visiting, or mingling in general society.

HINTS FOR DRESSING WELL.

1. CONSULT suitability of occasion, and where any doubt of the style of dress exists, avoid over-dressing. A little fault on the other side is preferable to this, as a lady may be more simply costumed than those around her, and appear to greater

advantage than if she is more showy in her apparel and ornaments than her companions.

2. Carefully select, in shopping, the best material you can
afford to purchase, rather than the most showy. A dress
made of good fabric, if it is only a domestic gingham, will not
only be more serviceable than any fabric made showily but
worthlessly, for mere effect.

3. In dressing for a picnic, water-party, croquet meeting, or
any other out-door gathering, select, when practicable, an attire that will wash. It is well, also, to be provided with a
waterproof cloak and hood, easily carried, and even if a little
troublesome while the sun shines, invaluable if a sudden
shower attacks the pleasure party.

4. Avoid carefully the *extreme* of the fashion. It is in far
better taste to moderate any extravagance of the capricious
goddess than to allow her to govern entirely every puff or
band. If bonnets are worn very small, do not aim to make
yours invisible. If they are to be large, it is not advisable to
rival the proportions of a market-basket.

5. Do not aim at eccentricity. A certain personality and
becomingness of attire should be studied, but utterly to ignore
the prevailing modes, is quite as apt to be a proof of a weak
mind as of a strong one. It is no sign of genius to wear a
long coat when every one else wears a short one, and the Bo-
hemian style is quite as apt to be aped by the empty-headed
as to be originated by the talented.

6. Avoid glaring contrasts, in color, material, or value. A
real lace shawl will look as badly over a cheap lawn dress as
a rich silk will under a coarse linen wrap.

7. Keep in scrupulous order your gloves, boots, and fine
linens, or laces. There is no surer proof of a slattern than
to see holes in the gloves, soiled collars or cuffs, or ill-fitting,
shabby boots. If your income will not allow kid gloves and
lace collars, wear cotton gloves and linen collars, but let
them fit nicely, and be always in exquisitely nice order. Be
sure a neat linen collar will more surely mark the lady than
a torn or soiled one of expensive lace.

8. Never wear any imitation finery. If real lace, real furs,
real velvets, and real jewelry are not at your command, wear
none at all. It is not a mark of gentility to appear in expensive ornaments or lace, but it is a mark of vulgarity to wear
what is only an imitation of a valuable article.

9. Cheap goods will generally be found an utter extravagance. If you pay for an article what it is fairly worth, you

have then a right to complain if it proves inferior to what was represented to you.

10. In selecting velvets and ribbons, examine the edge carefully. Inferior goods of this class will be found to have thin, broken edges, while those of first-rate quality are invariably firm and even.

11. In arranging trimming, always allow about three inches to the yard for corners and fullness. If a trimming is very elaborate, an even larger allowance will be found useful.

12. Goods that will turn, or which are exactly the same on both sides, will be found not only more easily altered or made over, but more economical in the first making.

13. Pattern dresses should be carefully selected, and bought only of reliable persons, as they are apt to prove utterly useless when cut, from deficiency of material, or bad management of the pattern.

14. Avoid glaring colors; they are becoming to but few, and always in bad taste, from being too conspicuous.

15. A traveling-dress should be quiet in color, strong in fabric, and simple in make.

16. Dresses made to be worn in a car, upon a boat, or in omnibuses, should be made to bear crushing well. Stiff material, elaborately ruffled or puffed, will present a lamentable contrast to its first freshness, after an hour's ride in a crowded omnibus. Soft woolens, whether thick or thin, stand this contact better than any other material, excepting a first-rate quality of silk.

17. In the selection of stockings, examine the heels. These are generally thin and poor when the hosiery is of an inferior quality. German and English hosiery, especially the latter, will be found most economical in the end, though the first outlay is larger than that for American goods.

18. Never force the season. The most exquisite and tasteful of spring attire will never appear well if worn too early in the season, on a windy March day, or under a threatening, gloomy sky. Even if the dress you would discard is somewhat worn, it will look better upon an unseasonable day than new finery worn too soon.

19. If you discard flannels in summer, always keep an intermediate suit to wear early in the fall and late in the spring, before assuming or rejecting your thicker ones. In a variable climate it is not only uncomfortable, but positively dangerous, to take off winter flannels at once, even on the warmest

day. Gauze merino, or Angolo flannel, is a good temporary substitute.

20. Ready-made garments should be examined carefully in all the seams, and especially at the end of the stitchings. Many who buy them find at the first washing that, while the main part of the sewing is in good order, the ends of every seam have given way, and present a slovenly appearance, with a prospect of hours given to repair what should last as long as the garment.

21. It is not safe to purchase goods which are very highly dressed. They will be often found of an inferior quality, and what at first seemed thickness or durability of material too often proves a trick of dressing.

22. In selecting boots, the foot will present a better appearance, and the boots will wear much better if full half an inch longer than the foot. Not only does a boot that is exactly a fit in length wear out soon at the most conspicuous place, but it ruins the shape of the foot, by forcing it to develop in its breadth what is crowded in length. This should be especially remembered in the purchase of children's boots or shoes, as a short boot in childhood will surely make an ugly foot in maturity.

23. Over-dressed children are as attractive as organ men's monkeys. At no time of life is simplicity of attire so beautiful as in childhood or youth.

24. Never wear jewelry in the street. Such articles as are necessary to keep the dress in order are admissible, but necklaces, bracelets, and rings in profusion are in excessively bad taste in walking attire.

25. Elaborate street dresses are in bad taste very early in the day, in dull, gloomy weather, or in errands and to markets, provision stores, or business places.

26. Evening-dresses should be purchased in establishments where they can be selected by artificial light. Colors and combinations that are exquisite by daylight, will often fail to be effective when under the blaze of a chandelier, or exposed to the test of wax-light.

27. In making evening-dresses, trimmings and ornaments should always be tested by the same artificial light in which they are to be worn. The effect of gas-light upon color is often very different from that of oil or candle-light.

28. Dull or neutral-colored gloves are generally in better taste than bright ones, unless the latter are worn in contrast to a somber-tinted dress. To have a bright glove to match a bright dress, is an abomination to the eyes of people of taste.

29. Colored boots, although they may be in fashion, are generally theatrical in effect, and seldom in good taste. They have also the disadvantage of being generally unbecoming to the foot.

30. It is only upon very full dress occasions that trimming is admissible about the feet. Huge bows or rosettes upon walking-boots are never pretty, even if fashionable. Neatly-fitting, plain walking-boots are in better taste.

31. It is unsafe as well as indelicate to adopt too far any fashion which exposes the neck in the street. Dresses cut low in front should only be worn in the house, even if fashion sanctions their appearance at the promenade.

32. Carriage-dresses may be more elaborate than those worn for walking. More delicate and costly fabrics will look well in a handsome barouche than can with propriety appear on the sidewalk.

33. Parasols should be selected with some attention to their becoming or unbecoming effect. A pallid face seen in the reflected light of a pale-green parasol will not look better than a florid, overheated one under a canopy of rose-color.

34. Be careful in altering an old garment into a new style that the material is worthy of promotion. It was rather tiresome to people of good taste to see how shabby some of the old shawls twisted into Arabs had become. It by no means follows that alteration in shape will renovate material.

35. Consult your figure as well as your face in the choice of your dress, and if you cannot follow the fashion without appearing ridiculous, modify the fashion.

36. In dressing the hair, be careful that it conforms to the style of the dress. An elaborate *coiffure* is in bad taste with an unpretending dress, while rich attire requires also some attention to head-dress, or arrangement of locks.

37. Linen for dresses must be of good quality to be useful at all. A poor linen suit is always a crushed, rumpled, untidy-looking raiment, and even the best is suitable only for travel, or an undress walking-attire.

38. Gentlemen should carefully avoid any conspicuous article of dress or jewelry. Nothing more surely marks a vulgar mind.

39. It is a good rule to buy corset-lacings of loosely-woven elastic cotton. These are as strong as the more firmly made, but will yield some to the movements of the figure, and keep

the corsets in better shape than where they are strained by every motion.

40. Satchels, and such small articles as are carried in the hand, as card-cases or porte-monnaies, can exhibit as much taste in their selection as any portion of the actual attire. We have seen a bright green porte-monnaie and a cuir-colored satchel lying upon a dress of blue silk, with what effect may be better imagined than described.

41. Feathers should only be worn in winter. They are as much out of place upon a summer hat or bonnet as fur would be upon a lace mantle.

42. Large ornaments are seldom becoming, unless upon a very tall or large woman. To see a little woman with an immense breast-pin, or a pair of enormous ear-rings, is simply absurd.

43. Jewels should be worn sparingly, should be only worn when genuine, and upon full-dress occasions, and should then carefully match the remainder of the attire.

44. Rich ornaments may sometimes relieve a simple dress, if neat and tasteful, but will never atone for a shabby or inappropriate one.

45. Cheap artificial flowers are simply hideous. Flowers to appear upon the costume of a well-dressed lady should be of the most exquisite finish, and finest quality. They are never a necessity, and when they cannot be procured of the choicest kind, had better be dispensed with altogether.

46. Refinement in feeling requires refinement in dress. A lady of delicacy will be found ever delicately and modestly attired.

47. The best silk to wear is the best quality of gros grain. It is also the richest and most superb in appearance, although not the most showy.

48. Cheap silk has the meanest appearance of any cheap goods. Silk is a luxury, and should always be of good quality. More inexpensive fabric will present a much better appearance than inferior silk, however showily it may be made or trimmed.

49. Embroidery should be carefully selected, and very fine. Coarse embroidery does not look well upon any garment, and upon any outside portion of the dress, is conspicuously tawdry, and in bad taste. If worn at all, it should be of the best.

50. Lace shawls are a luxury that cannot look well unless most expensive and elegant. Unless the income will warrant a variety of these wraps, they should be selected of shape and

pattern that will not soon become unfashionable. The regular shawl shape is the most economical, as that will never be out of style, and it has also the advantage of displaying the pattern effectively.

51. If thread lace cannot be purchased for shawls, llama lace is very rich and pretty for a substitute. Imitation lace should never be worn by any well-dressed lady.

52. In wearing short dresses, especially on the street, be careful that they are not too short. It is useless to adopt the style unless the dress clears the ground, but that object attained, it is not in good taste to expose the whole foot and ankle. A pretty foot does not look any better than an ugly one if too freely offered for criticism.

53. One of the most beautiful and useful of summer fabrics is a fine quality of linen lawn, and it has always the advantage of washing well.

54. It is as great an affectation for a young person to assume the dress of middle age, as it is for an elderly person to wear dress becoming and appropriate for a miss of sixteen. A certain gayety and brightness of attire is as suitable for youth as sober colors and quiet styles are for the more advanced in life.

55. Young persons should generally avoid the very heavy fabrics, even for full dress. Velvet, heavy silk, and rich satin are never so appropriate for the very young as the lighter silks and thinner fabrics, which have a certain airy grace suited to most festive occasions.

56. Seaside dresses must be selected to bear the contact with the spray, which ruins most colors and many fabrics. On this account white is the most serviceable, and generally becoming, in thick or thin goods. It is manufactured now in such variety of texture, from heavy piqué and marseilles to the thinnest of muslin, that almost an entire summer wardrobe may be made of it. It has also the merit of never fading, and being really renewed whenever it is done up. It is universally becoming, and can be varied by style of make and variety in ornament and trimming.

57. Wardrobes to be often packed should be made with as few ruffles and puffings as fashion will allow. It is difficult, even with all the modern improvements for packing, to retain the freshness of a dress after it has once been crowded into the limits of a trunk. Very expensive dresses may have the trimmings taken off, packed separately, and put on again after unpacking, with advantage.

58. A boot or glove that is too tight never makes the hand

or foot appear smaller, but, on the contrary, by forcing it to look compressed and strained, gives the impression that boots and gloves of attainable size are too small to fit it.

59. Earrings should not be worn too heavy. It is not unusual for these ornaments to tear the flesh by their weight, causing a permanent disfigurement that it is impossible either to remedy or to conceal. Light and tasteful ornaments of this kind are also more becoming than the very heavy or large ones. An ornament that is too large gives an impression of imitation or valueless material.

60. Diamonds and other glittering stones should never form a portion of the daylight attire of a well-dressed lady. They should be strictly confined to evening-dress, as they require artificial light for brilliancy, and are unsuited to any but the most dressy occasions.

61. Thin fabrics should be worn over silk, unless in wash material, when the under-dress should be of fine cambric or linen. Skirts of sheer book-muslin are the prettiest under lawn or such thin goods.

62. Trousseaus should be selected to look well for at least one season. It is almost impossible in the present often-changing fashions to arrange out-door attire for more than three months, but all excepting that portion of the wardrobe may be more bountifully provided.

63. There is no surer test of the taste of a lady than her usual morning attire at home. A neat and even elegant morning-dress is certain to be worn by the truly well-dressed lady, and the slattern will betray her untidy propensities more surely in that dress than in any other. It is not expedient for the lady who is busy during the morning hours to be expensively attired, but neatness and propriety of costume are never more apparent or appreciated than at the breakfast-table.

64. Very light gloves are only suitable for a very light or elaborate street-dress. They are more appropriate for an evening costume, an opera or concert-dress, but can be worn also with a summer street-suit, or a very dressy winter one.

65. A fan, when carried for full-dress, should never be in glaring contrast to the dress, or so bright as to destroy its effect. White or black are suitable for light or dark dresses, and white silk covered with black lace is the most useful of all fans. Bright colors in fans should be very sparingly used, though they are sometimes effective with a pure white or a black lace dress.

66. Contrast of color is one of the most difficult of all matters to manage tastefully. It is safer, as a general rule, to make a perfect match in trimmings and accompaniments, but a carefully-adjusted contrast is certainly better than an imperfect match. Two shades of one color are in very bad taste.

67. Never wear two bright colors at the same time. Somber or neutral tints may be effectively brightened by a gay knot of ribbon, or a flower, but never by two bright contrasting colors.

68. Traveling-dresses, when the season permits, should be made of wash material. Nothing is so tenacious and disagreeable as the dust contracted in travel, and once settled in woolen goods it is almost impossible entirely to dislodge it.

69. Two garments are indispensable in the wardrobe of a lady who travels much. A waterproof cloak with a large hood, and a full, loose, linen duster, to entirely cover the dress. Wet or dusty weather may be safely defied with these two garments. It is not always possible to tell which will be most required upon a long journey, but it is generally safest to have both where they can be conveniently unpacked.

70. Veils, although generally becoming, are often very trying to the eyesight, and unless really worn as a protection from dust, are better avoided.

71. It is best to avoid long floating ribbons in any crowded assembly. They will often be found a great care, and their beauty is entirely lost when you are limited for room.

72. Fine lace dresses, or evening-dresses of very thin and delicate fabric, should only be worn when there is a probability of plenty of space, as they will be greatly injured, if not entirely destroyed, by the pressure of a crowd. Silk, even if of very delicate color and style, will be found more serviceable in a very crowded ball or party-room.

73. A number of rings, even if they are all very valuable, are in bad taste. It appears like an ostentatious display of wealth to load the hands with expensive and conspicuous rings. One, of some valuable stone or rare workmanship, is all that should be worn.

74. It is always in bad taste to wear several kinds of precious stones. Two, happily contrasted in the same setting, will often happily contrast with each other, but unless combined in this way, even two kinds are in bad taste. If you wear diamonds, wear no other stones, and let the rule apply to other stones. Jewels, to be in good taste, must be worn in complete sets.

THE END.

THE
Great Wide Awake Library.

The Largest, Cheapest, and Best Library in the World.

ONLY FIVE CENTS.   ONLY FIVE CENTS.

FRANK TOUSEY, Publisher,

Box 2730.   34 and 26 North Moore St., N. Y.

SEND FOR A CATALOGUE.